ASTEROID CITY

also by Wes Anderson from Faber

RUSHMORE
THE ROYAL TENENBAUMS
MOONRISE KINGDOM
THE GRAND BUDAPEST HOTEL
ISLE OF DOGS
THE FRENCH DISPATCH

ASTEROID CITY

screenplay by
WES ANDERSON

story by
WES ANDERSON
ROMAN COPPOLA

faber

First published in 2023
by Faber & Faber Limited
The Bindery
51 Hatton Garden
London EC1N 8HN

First published in the USA in 2023

Typeset by Faber & Faber Limited
Printed and bound in the UK by TJ Books Limited

A CIP record for this book is available from the British Library

ISBN 978-0-571-38320-7

Printed and bound in the UK on FSC® certified paper in line with our continuing
commitment to ethical business practices, sustainability and the environment.
For further information see faber.co.uk/environmental-policy

2 4 6 8 10 9 7 5 3 1

Contents

Digging the Ditch

A conversation between WA (Wes Anderson, screenwriter, director), WD (Walter Donohue, guide), RC (Roman Coppola, screenwriter), JR (Jake Ryan, actor, playing Woodrow), JS (Jason Schwartzman, actor, playing Augie Steenbeck/Jones Hall)

WA Walter, are you guiding us through it?

WD To some extent. The last time most of us met was just before the release of *Isle of Dogs*, and we did a little conversation about that film which provided the introduction to the screenplay. Here we are again, a few years later.

WA Jake was a little boy in that movie.

JR I played the junior interpreter.

WD The three of you, Jason, Roman and Wes, were involved in the creation of this script. Is that right?

WA I think Roman and I wrote it.

WD Oh, okay.

WA But the movie was written for Jason. The movie begins with us saying: here's a character Jason has never played before, which draws on facets of what we know he is and can do, and we can build a whole movie around it. I'm now going to try to use the type of metaphor Jason would use, and it won't be as good as it would be if he was making it up, but I'm saying the place on the game board that says 'Start': it says 'Jason' on it.

JS That would be a great game, by the way. A screenplay-writing board game.

RC Write five pages. Advance three steps.

WA 'Lights, camera, action.' That could be the game. It begins with the script.

JS Pick a card: unforeseen weather, storm rolling in, *force majeure*.

WA Negative damage. Go back three spaces.

RC Scheduling conflict with actor.

WA Go to the commissary. Instead of jail.

JR Or that could also just be jail.

WD Which part is Jason playing?

WA Jason is Augie Steenbeck. Also called Jones Hall.

WD Would the script have been any different if Jason had been there while you were writing it?

WA No.

WD OK. One of the things I think is very interesting about the film is this issue of grief. Wes, I don't remember in your previous films where it played such an important part. It makes the film incredibly moving – how each of these characters relates to the death of the mother. The husband, the children, the father. It just suffuses everything, even though there are many other things going on in the film. Especially Stanley Zak, and how he comes to understand why the girls have to do what they do: burying the Tupperware rather than imposing his will on it. Somehow all the characters, that family, are brought together through their grief, and it gives the film a real emotional heft.

WA I guess maybe deaths: these are some of the biggest milestones in our lives. I think all of us can list these people just right off the top of our heads. These losses. That's what the movie's about, I think, possibly. The cosmic force of our lost people. (We thought about the Truffaut movie *The Green Room*.) At the end, Jason and Margot Robbie are playing two actors in a scene, but they're playing an imaginary scene that was cut out of a play that doesn't even exist. It's really a scene between this man and the woman who was the most important person in his life. Who is dead and gone. And, in a way, the whole movie is written just to get our way to this one conversation. And I don't even know what the conversation is. It's a visitation.

WD Can you imagine the script, the film, without that extra layer of the theatre?

WA Well, I could certainly imagine the trailer without it, because if you've watched the current cut of the trailer, you have no idea that any of it is in black and white, or that any parts of the movie are in the theatre at all. Because it's not in there.

JS I want to see the trailer.

WA Can I ask a question? What is grief? Jason, Roman, Jake: what is it, exactly?

JS I always think of the word 'grief' and the word 'mourning', those two. Grieving, mourning: in this form, it seems like you're actively going through it. Whereas 'grief' without the '-ing': it has a kind of stillness. I don't want to say stagnant, but like a non-moving heaviness.

WA It's a state. A world you've entered.

JS Yes. As opposed to you moving through it, it is surrounding you.

WA It's like water.

WD It's a dark cloak. Mourning seems to be something that happens after the event. Someone's died, and you're in a period of mourning that person. But grief, I think, is the aftermath of that. It envelops you. And, in some cases, it takes a long time for that cloak to be removed from your shoulders.

JS It's not unlike someone's scent that seems to stay in the fibres of a fabric for a long time. The person is gone, but there they are still in the pillow.

WA Joan Didion talks about her magical thinking. For a period of time, even though you can say, 'Yes, he's gone, she's gone,' your body, nevertheless, can't accept it. It changes the reality too much. You just can't believe it. There's no chance for a single conversation. Ever again. And how often you say: the only person who could really understand or who could tell me about this thing is gone. Like a city wiped away by an earthquake.

RC There are the joys of something coming into your life. Like a child. Filling up the well. And then the opposite. The extinguishing effect of losing someone. It seems like a cyclical human situation. Day, night. It's kind of a binary, these counterparts of life.

WA Well, you have two metaphors there. The birth, you call it, is filling something up. But you didn't say emptying. It's extinguishing. It doesn't just empty it out, it erases the whole container.

RC When you have a child, you enjoy them in the moment, but, as they grow, you think: what are we going to do for next Halloween? When they find a boyfriend or girlfriend. All the future that you project. And then on the opposite end: those things receding away. It's in the rear-view mirror, passing, but you're looking forward to what's unfolding. I do recall, Wes, when we first sat down, I remember, I feel like we were in the little blue room of your house in England . . .

WA The Morning Room.

RC The Morning Room (but it could have been the mourning room). I remember that little seminal beginning, whatever that was, when you're feeling a project starting to come to life, and in our process, you (Wes) have something that's this little seed that's beginning, and you're describing it, and I do remember that grief and loss. You began with: 'He's a widower.'

WA That was the beginning. This character for Jason, who's somebody who is arriving with this loss already, something's extinguished (or emptied). This is the state he's in when he enters. When he comes onto the stage.

RC Stage right.

JS Jake, what do you want to say?

JR I haven't experienced a lot of grief in my life, fortunately, at least not so far. But I've watched people experience grief and, from my point of view, it looks like it's mostly remembering certain points in time when they were there, and what it made them feel. Sometimes it can be the little things, like looking out of a window and remembering and finding some lost memory that was there that you haven't thought of in a while.

WA Remind me, because I remember during the movie: was it your aunt?

JR Yes, it was my aunt. It was her heart. It's very strange because it was almost like we were grieving before she had actually died. We all had a feeling that she wasn't going to make it and when she finally died, it was like a lot of pent-up stress and maybe a little bit of catharsis at the end. Just releasing all of that. Sometimes grief is a powerful motivator. It can inspire you to change things or create things. That's what I want to say.

WA For me, Jake: well, you see, my father died recently. It's two months ago.

JR Oh, I'm sorry to hear that.

WA He was ninety, and he sort of died over a very long period of time, because he had dementia, and he was incapacitated, so it was a slow process. And I find, in a way, the process of literally saying goodbye to him, this was a very powerful thing. This was a slightly overwhelming experience of literally saying goodbye to him while he was alive. And his death was more like, it wasn't the end of the grief, but it was a lighter experience than the process of saying goodbye. On the other hand, there are people I think about often, such as Anjelica Huston's husband, Robert Graham, who died, not suddenly, not in an accident, but his illness was quick, and it was harsh, and it was unexpected. We lost him over a short period of time, and he was far from ready to go. Or another one I think of is Earl McGrath, who was old, but he was full of life, you know, the day before he died. Earl fell. Over the last ten years, so many of my older friends, my friends who are twenty years older than me, twenty-five years older than me, thirty years older than me, I've lost most of them, along with my father. You enter a new part of your life when you join the others in that experience. Jason, you lost your father at such a young age. And I think that is a part of your view of life. It's informed by that. I would say some wisdom comes from that experience, at that young age. Some wisdom carries on.

JS Something surreal: when I read the script for the first time, to go back to the beginning, I was aware Wes and Roman were writing it, but then when it arrived, I sat down and read where Augie tells his son and his three daughters in the middle of this road trip west, he tells them his wife, their mother, has died. Well, without [Wes] knowing it, that's exactly what happened in my family, to my father. His mother died of breast cancer, and my grandfather didn't tell my father or his younger brother. Their father simply didn't know how to handle it. They moved from New York to Los Angeles, drove across the country, and, at some point during that trip, it was revealed that she was not on vacation somewhere but instead had died a few weeks before. I even found letters of my dad's asking this other person he knew, saying: Where was I the day of the funeral? What was I doing? What was I doing while everyone was at the funeral of my mother which I didn't know about.

WA How old were Jack and Uncle Leonard?

JS I think twelve and ten.

WA Twelve and ten. Oh, my gosh. Crazy. But you said to me and Roman, immediately, you said, 'This happened to my family.' And Roman, you didn't know that, right?

RC I didn't know that story. I vaguely knew that he had suffered a loss as a young man. But that's it. I didn't know that story.

WA What year do you think that was?

JS 1950.

RC There you go. Magical.

JS Isn't that interesting? It does seem like, in that era, like a cell phone in a movie or a type of car, it's an indicator of the time period, what time we might be in. I think talk about death or how to handle death is also a little marker. The way it was handled in 1950 might be different. It almost put me back into that time more than anything: this was handled in this way, a less modern approach to grief and death and how to talk about it with your family, and parenting. More like: bury it. I think it's interesting.

RC It's curious. I was going to say in my family, my mom, her dad died when she was a little girl, seven years old and, similarly, he sort of went away, and it was not spoken of. And she has a very searing memory when it was really at the end, they sort of kept it all away from the kids. And then at the very end, she was brought in to say goodbye, in effect, and it kind of scarred her, I think, because he was emaciated, you know, he was right at the very end moment.

WA She didn't know what was going on.

RC She didn't know what was going on. So it was a big wound for her. But it's curious, because, in the past, you feel like, growing up on a farm, you see life, you see death, you see kittens being born, or your dog dies, and there are wakes and dead bodies in your living room and so on. I guess it depends on your culture, but the kind of American, suburban, post-war time may have had some manner in which the culture decided that everything's great and not to share that type of news.

WA Also: they started making very bad food.

RC People moved out of the cities into the suburbs. Everything's kind of sunny and happy. Plastic life.

WA We close a curtain over death, and we're eating baloney. I know you like the fried baloney, Roman, but the baloney sandwich is not considered a better quality of food. Whatever your people were eating back in Sicily, I think it was probably better.

JS We went from processing death to processing food. You know, another thing, too, is Augie being a war photographer: I found it interesting that someone who's surrounded by death and violence and has probably seen some pretty intense stuff, doesn't know how to deal with it when it's his own family. When it's not in a war. You're photographing explosions, and you've made that a part of your life, and then, all of a sudden, it's in your own home, and now you've got to actually go through it.

WD Yes. For him, in this new context, how does he find the words?

WA At one point, Roman and I decided all the men in the movie each needed a pistol. We started giving people guns; but Augie is different because Augie has a clinical approach. The story is filled with all these men who probably came back from Europe not so many years ago, and they were in a place where people were getting blown up. Jeffrey Wright has a speech about what he experienced over these decades. There's something about this period in America where the country is prospering but maybe it has post-traumatic stress disorder, too.

JS It's in grief.

WA Maybe that's it. Maybe the country is in a state of grief. Even though the number of backyards in America between 1945 and 1955 has grown by a factor of twenty-five or something. The country is filled with all these plots where someone has plunked down a house. But maybe there's a little invisible dark cloud over each of them.

JS In the movie we explore grief, also, from the children's point of view, and the spouse's point of view, and the father's point of view. What must it be like to lose your mother? What does it feel like to lose your wife? What does it feel like to lose your daughter? That is the sort of campfire that they're all around; it's the log they bring to that fire.

WD Wes, what you were just saying about all these houses being built up in the suburbs. That was like the kind of house I grew up in in New Jersey. Our family lived on the bottom floor of the house. In the upper part, there was a woman with her child who was kind of my age at the time, about six or seven, and no father. And when I asked what had happened, where was the father, they said he was in Pearl Harbor. He was on one of those ships, and he died. Suddenly, like you say, the cloud came in above the family above us. This family that was no longer a family.

WA Ah. Two words is all you need. Pearl Harbor. You never think of a pearl, do you? You don't even really think of the harbor. I wonder, if you go back, was it probably some magical cove? Where you would dive in the clear waters, and there were reefs that were alive and beautiful.

RC You cut from pearl diving to dive bombing.

WA Were there kamikazes at Pearl Harbor?

RC I believe that was the primary way. I was watching a documentary on John Ford not long ago. He's kind of grouchy in this interview. It was a British TV guy. John Ford says making a movie is like digging a ditch, and you just hope that the earth is soft. When you're getting into it, you want some soft earth. Well, when we're writing a script, we're digging our ditch, and we hope the earth is soft, but you just keep digging, either way. We're very practical. It's fun, two years later, to sit back and examine some of the thoughts and themes that were latent, but almost never discussed again after the very beginning.

WA We have talked about grief in our lives, the three of us. Sorry not to include Jake in that combination, but we're so much older, and we three have spent so many years together talking about everything. Well, when we're working on a story for a movie, and now we've done a bunch of those together, we're digging our ditch, and we have our tasks to do, and we have construction work to do. But the difference with the ditch digging is that our construction job is about trying to make some kind of big poem that lasts for ninety-five minutes, and when you start digging you don't actually know what it *is*. Self-expression is not usually part of what we are attempting, except that usually it is part of what gives you the impetus to bother to try it in the first place. This is why the self-expression is usually not *expressed*. It's more about: 'We want to make something,' but I guess underneath the whole reason to make something is because you feel you have to, and that's the result of something else.

WD Shall we end there? That sounds like the end.

Cast and Credits

Augie Steenbeck	Jason Schwartzman
Midge Campbell	Scarlett Johansson
Stanley Zak	Tom Hanks
General Gibson	Jeffrey Wright
Dr. Hickenlooper	Tilda Swinton
The Host	Bryan Cranston
Conrad Earp	Edward Norton
Schubert Green	Adrien Brody
J. J. Kellogg	Liev Schreiber
Sandy Borden	Hope Davis
Roger Cho	Stephen Park
June Douglas	Maya Hawke
The Motel Manager	Steve Carell
The Mechanic	Matt Dillon
Polly	Hong Chau
Saltzburg Keitel	Willem Dafoe
The Actress/Wife	Margot Robbie
The Aide-de-camp	Tony Revolori
Woodrow	Jake Ryan
Dinah	Grace Edwards
Clifford	Aristou Meehan
Shelly	Sophia Lillis
Ricky	Ethan Lee
The Alien	Jeff Goldblum

Directed by
Wes Anderson

Screenplay by
Wes Anderson

Story by
Wes Anderson
Roman Coppola

Produced by
Wes Anderson
Steven Rales
Jeremy Dawson

Executive Producers
Roman Coppola
Henning Molfenter
Christoph Fisser
Charlie Woebcken

Director of Photography
Robert Yeoman, A.S.C.

Production Designer
Adam Stockhausen

Costume Designer
Milena Canonero

Film Editor
Barney Pilling, A.C.E.

Additional Editor
Andrew Weisblum, A.C.E.

Music by
Alexandre Desplat

Music Supervisor
Randall Poster

Hair and Make-up Designer
Julie Dartnell

Co-Producers
Octavia Peissel
John Peet

Casting
Douglas Aibel, C.S.A.

Line Producer
Frédéric Blum

Associate Producer
Molly Rosenblatt

First Assistant Director
Atilla Salih Yücer

Second Unit Director
Martin Scali

Animatic/ Title Sequence Editor
Edward Bursch

Storyboard Artist
Jay Clarke

Script Supervisor
Jennifer Furches

Key Grip
Sanjay Sami

First Assistant Camera
Vincent Scotet

Unit Manager
Bertrand Girard

Prop Master
Sandy Hamilton

Stand-by Prop Masters
Mike Drury
Benoît Herlin

Sound Mixer
Valentino Giannì

Re-recording Mixer/Supervising Sound Editors
Wayne Lemmer
Chris Scarabosio

Original Music Orchestrated and Conducted By
Conrad Pope

Music Editor
Robin Baynton

Original Music Recorded and Mixed By
Simon Rhodes

Graphic Designer
Erica Dorn

Colorist
Gareth Spensley

A S T E R O I D
C I T Y

CAST OF PRINCIPAL CHARACTERS

HOST

CONRAD EARP (playwright)

AUGIE STEENBECK/JONES HALL (war photographer/actor)

WOODROW (Augie's son)

MIDGE CAMPBELL/MERCEDES FORD (movie star/actress)

DINAH (Midge's daughter)

STANLEY ZAK (Augie's father-in-law)

GRIF GIBSON (five-star general)

DR. HICKENLOOPER (astronomer)

JUNE (school teacher)

MONTANA/ASQUITH EDEN (cowboy/actor)

J.J. KELLOGG (advertising executive)

CLIFFORD (J.J.'s son)

SANDY BORDEN (Cookie Troopers regional headmistress)

SHELLY/LUCRETIA SHAVER (Sandy's daughter/actress)

ROGER CHO/LINUS MAO (architect/actor)

RICKY (Roger's son)

MECHANIC/WALTER GERONIMO (mechanic/actor)

MOTEL MANAGER (entrepreneur)

SCHUBERT GREEN (theatre director)

POLLY (Schubert's wife)

AIDE-DE-CAMP (to the General)

DRIVER/BODYGUARD (to Midge Campbell)

ALIEN

INT. TELEVISION STUDIO. EVENING

Black and white.

A 1950's-era broadcast soundstage. Cameras on pneumatic pedestals. Microphones on telescoping booms. A team of technicians encircling the studio floor. The lights come up on our host, Brylcreemed in a dark suit and necktie. He addresses the audience:

HOST
Tonight's program takes us backstage to witness first-hand the creation, start to finish, of a new play mounted on the American stage.

The lights change to reveal the "theatre district" of a miniature metropolis: skyscrapers, streetlights, a canyon of box-office marquees.

HOST
"Asteroid City" does not exist. It is an imaginary drama created expressly for this broadcast. The characters are fictional, the text hypothetical, the events an apocryphal fabrication -- but together they present an authentic account of the inner-workings of a modern theatrical production.

The metropolis splits in two, sliding open like a curtain as the host continues:

HOST
Our story begins, of course, with an ink ribbon.

Revealed behind the moving scenery: a man (middle-aged, balding, in a cowboy/western-style dressing gown with embroidered lassos and bedroom slippers with jingling decorative spurs) hunts and pecks at a typewriter.

HOST
Conrad Earp, playwright, native of upper Wyoming. Well-known for his romantic/poetic tapestries of life west of the Rocky Mountains.

The playwright sips at a highball then continues to type at some length before the host finally interjects:

HOST
There is little amusement to be had, however, in watching a man type. Skip
(more)

HOST (cont'd)
ahead, then, past the lonely, agonized months of composing, revising, polishing, editing, rewriting, cutting, pasting, pacing, doodling, and solitary drinking --

The lights change again to reveal a full-scale, intricately decorated theatre proscenium with curtains, footlights, and a constellation of chalk-arrows and tape-marks zig-zagging across the boards. Stagehands criss-cross carrying sofas and tables, raising and lowering sandbags, removing the playwright's typewriter and chair, etc.

HOST
-- and join our company as they take the stage for their first read-through rehearsal. Location: the Tarkington Theatre, 345 South Northwest Avenue.

The host exits. The stagehands clear the floor and wait. The room falls quiet. The playwright, center-stage, now holds in his hands the manuscript for his completed play. He looks to the audience; he looks to the wings; he clears his throat; he begins to read:

PLAYWRIGHT
Curtain rises on a desert bus-stop halfway between Parched Gulch and Arid Plains.

The playwright gestures to various as-yet-unconstructed scenic elements and installations.

PLAYWRIGHT
Main scenography includes: a twelve-stool luncheonette, a one-pump filling station, and a ten-cabin motor-court hotel.

In the nearby wings: stagehands listen next to racks of ropes and pulleys; electricians listen next to rows of sockets and fuses; a property master silently inventories his kit.

PLAYWRIGHT
Up-stage left: the Tomahawk Mountains (highest peak: 11,000 feet). Up-stage right: an unfinished highway overpass which vaults up twenty feet then chops off mid-air behind a permanent road-block. Down-front: an impact crater a hundred feet in depth and diameter encircled by a low Little League-variety chainlink fence. Off-stage, distant: a 650-car freight train which click-clacks by at five miles an hour. Note to chief electrician:

Up above: a stagehand on a catwalk listens as he operates a spot.

PLAYWRIGHT

The light of the desert sun is neither warm nor cool, but always <u>clean</u> -- and, above all: unforgiving.

The playwright introduces the players, an assembly of professional actors and actresses, not in costume/not in character, several in their early teens. They periodically flip the pages of their dog-eared scripts, pencilling notes.

First: a handsome, compact actor, T-shirt with sweater tied around the waist, brush-cut hairdo, in a folding chair turned backwards; a reedy boy fidgeting beside him.

PLAYWRIGHT

Cast: Augie Steenbeck, war photographer, early forties. His son, Woodrow, fourteen (also known as “Brainiac”).

Next: a brunette actress in discreet, precise make-up, hands in lap, seated bolt upright in a pencil-skirt and tailored jacket; a bobby-soxer filing her nails beside her.

PLAYWRIGHT

Midge Campbell, late-thirties, film actress. Her daughter, Dinah, fifteen.

Next: a blowsy/smudged actress with an unsuccessful permanent; a former professional quarterback.

PLAYWRIGHT

June Douglas, schoolteacher. Grif Gibson, five-star-general.

Next: an actor in a cardigan sweater; an actor in a sailor’s peacoat; an actress in a woolen cap; more teenagers (among them a short-haired gamine in black turtleneck, tights, and leotard).

PLAYWRIGHT

J.J. Kellogg, Roger Cho, Sandy Borden; Clifford, Ricky, Shelly.

Finally: a man-about-town in last night’s dinner jacket, overcoat, and patent-leather shoes. He sits with his legs crossed, at ease.

PLAYWRIGHT

Stanley Zak, sixty-five, retired.

The lights dim once more. The playwright pauses before he concludes with reserved drama:

PLAYWRIGHT
The action of the play takes place in September of 1955. Act I. Friday morning, 7am. Act II. The next day. Act III. One week later.

Lights fade to black. Silence.

TITLE SEQUENCE:

Widescreen/color.

A super-extended freight train rolls along rusty tracks, curving through canyons and mesas, chugging over trusses and trestles. The engineer leans from a locomotive window, pulling his whistle. A pilotman rides seated on the caboose platform with his feet on an iron step-stool. The brakeman squats perched on the roof of a boxcar, rolling a cigarette.

Cargo: stacked Pontiacs; white gravel; horses and cattle; avocados, pecans, grapefruits, almonds, artichokes; a tractor and a bulldozer; a tank wagon of raw milk; and a short-range ballistic missile labeled:

10 Megaton Nuclear Warhead
Caution: DO NOT DETONATE
without Presidential Approval

EXT. HIGHWAY. DAY

A warning bell rings at a railroad crossing.

The train slowly rattles over a blacktop interstate which descends, sidewinding, from a distant plateau down to a concise desert town circumvented by towering cactus, yucca, and sagebrush. Dry winds blow red dust and tangled scrub. A roadrunner darts and sprints. In the remote background: a range of faraway mountains encircling the vast, sandy arena. In the close foreground: a decorative covered-wagon roadside sign which reads "Asteroid City, Pop. 87" in carved orange letters.

The town itself: a café, a motel, a gas station. A parked Chrysler sedan, a Ford with a running board. White, wooden, ranch-style fencing punctuated by telephone poles, electric wires, and palm trees in tight clusters. A few barns and bungalows dot the outskirts, along with a billboard advertising an Indian reservation casino 250 miles ahead.

On the edge of the town: the ruins of the uncompleted/chopped-off elevated highway-spur with an official roadblock warning:

Route-Calculations Error
RAMP CLOSED INDEFINITELY
Department of Roads and Rails

A hundred yards into the desert: a modestly-sized astronomical observatory; a field of small radio telescopes; a chainlink fence with regional-monument/point-of-interest marker; a flight of steep, skinny wooden steps which descends into a wide crater with, at center, ensconced in a rebar display-cage: a pock-marked metallic rock the size of a cantaloupe.

EXT. AUTO GARAGE. DAY

The filling station. A hanging sign gently creaks. "Ice, Tires, Service." The roadrunner trots to the center of the road and sniffs at a sun-dried (dead) snake. A hazy speck shimmers-up over a rise down the highway. The bird watches, then jolts back into the brush. The speck, as it approaches, takes the form of a sand-beaten tow-truck pulling a wood-paneled station wagon in its winch. The brief convoy pulls under the shade of the fuel-pump awning and crunches to a stop.

Four doors open (two on the cab, two on the wagon), and release a weary, sweaty group which includes: a small man in his early forties, bearded, dressed in a safari jacket with a Swiss camera around his neck. He is Augie. A gangly boy, fourteen, dressed in Bermuda shorts and tinted plastic sun-visor labeled: "Brainiac." He is Woodrow. Three girls with matted hair, aged four, five, and six, dressed in a mixed combination of bathing suits, pixie costumes, pajamas, ruby slippers, etc. They are Andromeda, Pandora, and Cassiopeia.

(NOTE: we recognize various performers as they appear in the story, now costumed and in-character, from their earlier introduction in the teleplay broadcast.)

A grizzled mechanic/tow-truck driver dressed in a grease-speckled overall jumpsuit powers up his winch, lowering the station wagon with a clanking rumble.

Woodrow scribbles in a small notebook. The three girls wander vaguely in a daze, whispering and humming. Augie sticks a pipe into his mouth, produces a Zippo lighter from one of his numerous pockets, and fuels it straight from the gasoline pump. He lights his pipe and puffs.

(NOTE: throughout the story, Augie employs an excess of self-conscious/actorly business: with his pipe, with his lighter, with his camera, with his beard, etc.)

INT. LUNCHEONETTE. DAY

A narrow, checkered-tile, chrome-and-bakelite café with soda fountain, chalkboard specials, and a short-order window communicating to the kitchen. Slatted blinds paint light/shadow stripes over the long counter. Country music plays on the jukebox. A chime jingles as Augie, Woodrow, and the three girls enter. The door clatters shut. A trapped fly buzzes against the screen.

Behind the counter, two women: a sun-spotted cashier in her sixties seated behind the register; and a Key-lime-green-uniformed waitress in her seventies thumbing through a Sears catalogue. They both look up at the arriving family. Augie says (almost inaudible) in a faintly old-Brooklyn accent:

AUGIE
Five orders of flapjacks and a black coffee.

The waitress nods and directs the group to sit. They occupy their stools, side-by-side. A lanky cook, forty, in a white cap and apron, snatches down the order-slip and peers out from the kitchen. Augie says bluntly:

AUGIE
Who needs to pee?

The girls respond with an adamant, unconvincing chorus: "Not me." "I don't." "Nobody needs to pee." Woodrow looks up from his notebook and says, matter-of-fact:

WOODROW
Our average speed is eighty-three feet per second. Poor fuel efficiency due to excess wind resistance. (Probably the luggage rack.) Based on data before the loss of power, obviously.

Augie nods, weary. Woodrow resumes his scribbling. The sisters mix a potion of salt, pepper, and mustard in an ashtray as they whisper sinister incantations. The waitress interjects:

WAITRESS
What do you little princesses want to drink?

The sisters respond suddenly, more or less in unison:

ANDROMEDA
We're not princesses.

CASSIOPEIA
I'm a vampire.

PANDORA
I'm a mummy in Egypt who got buried alive and came back to life with his head chopped off.

CASSIOPEIA
I suck people's blood.

ANDROMEDA
I'm a fairy.

Pause. The waitress says agreeably:

WAITRESS
How about a glass of strawberry milk?

A distant boom shudders the building. Augie and Woodrow frown. Augie says, alarmed:

AUGIE
What was that?

CASHIER
(inevitably)
Another atom bomb test.

Augie hesitates. He leans out the open window (followed by Woodrow). Fifty miles away, beyond the mountains: a massive mushroom cloud billows up into the sky. Augie's eyes widen. He holds up his camera and snaps a photograph.

INT. AUTO GARAGE. DAY

The station wagon is now hoisted up on a hydraulic repair-lift. The mechanic, Augie, Woodrow, and the three girls look up from below the vehicle into the grease-and-dirt-coated agglomeration of pipes, shafts, wires, and widgets. The mechanic explains:

MECHANIC
I've seen this combination of symptoms twice before in the '52 Estate Model. In one case, it was a quick fix of a 75 cent part. In the other case, it was a difficult, costly, time-consuming disassembly and remantling of the entire drivetrain and lubrication mechanism which didn't work. The motor exploded itself, and the body was stripped and sold for scrap. (There it is.)

The mechanic points to the corroded remains of a similar-model station wagon in a small junkyard next door. Augie frowns.

AUGIE
Which one've we got?

MECHANIC
We're about to find out.

The mechanic opens a small cardboard box and removes a fresh, clean, hexagonal nut. He displays it briefly to the group. He steps up onto a footstool and reaches up to carefully fit the nut onto the end of a threaded post. He slowly twists. Augie and the children move closer to watch. The mechanic twists tighter and tighter. He pauses to switch to a wrench. He gently twists until the nut resists, then gives it a little extra goose. He looks down at the group. He descends from the footstool and climbs up into the station wagon. He inserts the car key. He looks down at the group again. A hopeful nod. Augie watches, anxious.

The mechanic turns on the ignition, and the motor whirs to life.

MECHANIC
You got the first one.

AUGIE
(relieved)
How much do I owe you?

MECHANIC
Nothing. Ten dollars for the tow.

At that instant, simultaneously: both the vehicle's twin mufflers/exhaust tailpipes backfire and explode with a muted, concussive thud; all four tires spontaneously blow-out and drain flat, hissing; the engine seizes and goes dead; and a sizable, oil-coated, mechanical assembly (cast-iron, rubber-gasketed) drops free from the undercarriage into the drip-basin below where it sputters, vibrates, gasps, and squeals faintly, scooting and hopping nervously in the shallow viscosity. Augie asks, stunned:

AUGIE
What's that?

The mechanic stares, intrigued and slightly frightened, from the driver's seat above. He says quietly:

MECHANIC
I don't know.

The mechanic quickly descends. He sprays down the assembly with a high-pressure hose until it ceases its seizure. Augie and the children watch in perplexed amazement. Silence.

MECHANIC
I think you got a third problem we've never seen before.

EXT. HIGHWAY. DAY

A free-standing telephone booth next to a fence-post in the corner of a vacant plot between the gas station and the motel entrance. Bits of rubble and bottle-caps litter the dry, cracked earth. A single wire extends diagonally up from the top of the booth to an overhead line. Augie waits with the receiver to his ear.

(Woodrow lingers nearby scribbling periodically in his notebook while his three sisters run in circles singing eerily and swirling soap bubbles into the air with plastic wands).

SPLIT-SCREEN:

On one side: the interior of the telephone booth with chipped paint and pencil-graffitied numbers with abbreviated exchange-names. On the other side: the vast, wood-and-stone, low-ceiling living room of a luxurious ranch house overlooking a golf course. A houseboy in a yellow butler's jacket answers:

HOUSEBOY
Zak residence.

AUGIE
Romulus, this is Augie Steenbeck.

HOUSEBOY
Good morning, Mr. Augie. The gate is open.

AUGIE
We're not there.

HOUSEBOY
(mildly surprised)
You're not here?

The houseboy checks his watch and frowns.

AUGIE
May I speak to Mr. Zak?

HOUSEBOY
Yes, Mr. Augie.

The houseboy sets down the telephone and hurries away from camera, through the deep room, out via louvered double-doors. Augie mops his brow with a handkerchief.

Faintly: the sounds of a siren and a distant motor. Augie leans out of the booth and squints. Camera pans away, down the highway, to a black Chevy sedan roaring toward, whizzing past, then racing away from the telephone booth -- followed immediately by a state trooper in pursuit, lights flashing. A few exchanged gunshots pop. Camera continues panning (now 360 degrees) back to Augie watching, perturbed. (Woodrow, in the background, adds this event to his notebook.)

In the meantime: a tall, silver-haired seventy-year-old dressed in tartan trousers and clacking, spiked golf shoes enters the living room followed by the houseboy and approaches the telephone. He carries a tumbler of orange juice. He is Stanley. He picks up the receiver.

STANLEY
You're not here?

AUGIE
We're not there. The car exploded. Come get the girls.

STANLEY
(surprised)
The car -- exploded?

AUGIE
Parts of the car. Exploded itself, yes. Come get the girls.

STANLEY
(stiffening)
I'm not the chauffeur. I'm the grandfather. Where are you?

AUGIE
Asteroid City. Farm-route Six, mile 75. Come get the girls. I have to stay here with Woodrow.

STANLEY
(perplexed)
What are you talking about?

AUGIE
(irritated)
The thing. For Woodrow. We're there.

Augie motions obliquely to the motel: a classic motor court with individual clapboard bungalows. A sign next to the entrance reads: "Welcome, Junior Stargazers and Space Cadets!"

STANLEY
Hm.

Silence. Stanley says grimly:

STANLEY
How'd they take it?

AUGIE
(reluctant)
They didn't.

STANLEY
(puzzled)
No?

AUGIE
No.

STANLEY
(in disbelief)
No!

AUGIE
Yes.

Augie and Stanley say simultaneously, almost inaudibly:

STANLEY
You didn't tell them. Still.

AUGIE
I still didn't tell them.

STANLEY
(frustrated)
You promised.

AUGIE
I know.

Augie stares into space. He closes his eyes and shakes his head.

AUGIE
The time is never right.

Stanley nods slowly. He shares his advice, firm but philosophical:

STANLEY
The time is always wrong.

Augie contemplates this. Stanley asks, less important/aside:

STANLEY
Are you OK?

AUGIE
(lightly)
No.

Silence. Both men begin to quietly, almost imperceptibly, cry. Augie says -- just now realizing:

AUGIE
You never liked me, did you?

STANLEY
(more precisely)
I never <u>loved</u> you.

Augie nods. They both expand on the point:

AUGIE
You always thought I wasn't good enough for her.

STANLEY
I always thought she could've done better.

STANLEY
(pleased)
Yes. We're saying the same thing.

Augie takes a deep breath. Stanley drinks his orange juice, then gives two orders (one to the houseboy, one to Augie):

STANLEY
Gas up the Cadillac. Tell the kids.

AUGIE
I will.

HOUSEBOY
OK.

STANLEY
I'll be there when I get there.

Augie and Stanley bluntly hang up. Woodrow and his sisters stand next to Augie, alongside the telephone booth, waiting. Augie opens the door and looks into the near distance. Pause. He takes a photograph, then says:

AUGIE
It's the end of that car.

Augie begins to march across the highway. He issues clipped instructions as Woodrow and his sisters follow behind him:

AUGIE
Andromeda: check under the floor mats.
Pandora: check the side pockets.
Cassiopeia: check the cracks between the seats. Take everything.
(aside)
What do you think, Woodrow?

WOODROW
I think it's kind of sad.

Camera pans to the station wagon, now parked outside the garage on its four flat tires. The mechanic continues to examine it. Augie approaches the vehicle, steps up onto the rear bumper, and disconnects a roof-rack strap. He pulls down valises and camera cases, handing them to Woodrow, who lines them up in a row. The three sisters open doors and windows and begin to throw things out onto the ground, haphazard: bags, boxes, cartons; half-naked dolls and stuffed animals; partially-uneaten snacks, stray socks, books, etc.

Augie opens the glove box and withdraws: gloves, a packet of pipe-tobacco, a selection of maps and documents, and an old roll of exposed 120mm film. He flips open the passenger-side ashtray. He pauses. He stares. He bites his lip.

INSERT:

A cigarette butt smudged with red lipstick.

CUT TO:

A high-angle view of the entire, compact municipality. Augie, Woodrow, and the three girls re-cross the highway (heading to the motel) lugging their suitcases, bags, and boxes. From one direction: a trio of assorted station wagons enters the town, followed immediately by an Army Jeep tugging a small, steel-and-rivet trailer. From the other direction: two more station wagons, plus a cross-country bus which stops in front of the luncheonette.

EXT. LUNCHEONETTE/MOTEL. DAY

The door of the bus flings open. The driver, burly, in cap and uniform, descends first and shouts:

BUS DRIVER
Rest stop!
(checking his watch)
Thirteen minutes.

The bus driver ambles around to the nose of the bus, withdraws a wax paper-wrapped ham sandwich from his pocket, and takes a bite. Assorted passengers without baggage (a traveling salesman, a small church group with collared minister, an old man with two canes, a posse of cowboys and ranch hands) spill out and spread in various directions to stretch their legs, use the bathrooms (entrance on the outside of the building), smoke cigars/ cigarettes, and dart into the luncheonette. The screened door bangs open and shut repeatedly, chiming, as hamburger-coffee-and-doughnut-orders are called out in urgent voices. Finally, a class of ten eight-year-old pupils accompanied by two elderly-lady chaperones emerges from the bus carrying small suitcases and a picnic basket with, behind them: a seasoned but youthful schoolteacher. She wears a cardigan with knitted flowers stitched to it, a white collar, hair sharply parted, heels. She is June. One of the cowboys (name: Montana) briefly sidles back into frame to discreetly give her the once-over.

June stops the group as they reach the ground, announcing:

JUNE
Head count! Boys and girls?

The children immediately gather close and look up at June as each chirps his/her number, one to ten. June nods officiously.

JUNE
Plus Libby, Margie, and me. All present. Let's give thanks for a safe journey. Billy?

The children briskly fold their hands and bow their heads. A freckled boy improvises:

FRECKLED BOY
Dear Heavenly Father, We thank Thee kindly for a terrific bus ride. I ate three boxes of Crackerjacks and got a dog-whistle and a miniature map of the original thirteen colonies. Also: we saw a coyote get run over by a fourteen-wheeler, and it left him flat as a pancake. Boy, oh, boy! What else? The bus driver had to stop twice because Bernice couldn't hold it.

A girl with curly red hair opens her eyes and interjects sharply:

CURLY-HAIRED GIRL
Could so!

JUNE
(loudly)
Amen.

"Amens" all around; then June calls out, commanding but pleasant:

JUNE
Lunchtime! Line up single-file.

(NOTE: an increasing traffic of criss-crossing people appear in the foreground and background of this scene, welcoming arriving parties, preparing accommodations, rushing.)

Car doors swing open and whang shut as families disembark from the newly-arrived station wagons parked at various angles between the luncheonette and the motel. First: a strikingly blonde woman in her mid-thirties, glamorous in dark sunglasses, accompanied by her gum-chewing fifteen-year-old daughter. They are Midge and Dinah. Their driver/bodyguard is a tall, burly man in chinos and a blazer. His eyes scan left and right, checking security. Midge says, perspiring:

MIDGE
My word! It's hot.

DINAH
(shrugs)
It's the desert. What'd you expect?

MIDGE
Well, I don't know if I expected one thing or another -- but I'm wilting like a cut petunia.

Next: a businessman in his late forties, summer suit, straw hat tipped back, accompanied by his son, fourteen, in tennis clothes. They are J.J. and Clifford. Clifford plucks a tiny, bright red pepper from a vine on a trellis outside the luncheonette and holds it up to his father:

CLIFFORD
You dare me?

J.J.
(absently)
Dare you what?

CLIFFORD
(brightly)
To eat this hot pepper. It's an experiment.

J.J.
No.

Clifford bites the pepper in half. J.J. waits.

Next: a woman, forty-five, accompanied by her daughter, fourteen, both in brown-and-white gingham girl scout-type uniforms (labeled "Cookie Troopers"). They are Sandy and Shelly. Sandy wears a badge which reads "Regional Headmistress" and nibbles from a carton of Cookie Trooper Jam-Crispies. (She keeps a box of this kind in hand at all times throughout the story.) Shelly carries a movie magazine ("Screen Dreamboats") tucked under her arm. She whispers to her mother, furtive but awestruck, peering back past the other families:

SHELLY
Holy Toledo. That's Midge Campbell.

SANDY
(alerted)
Where? Who?

SHELLY
Right smack in back of you. Don't look.

Next: inside the open front window of the motor court check-in office, the motel manager (tall, rangy, amiable, in a bolo tie and Western shirt) greets a scientist (fifty, Hawaiian shirt/white trousers) accompanied by his aviator-spectacled son, fifteen. They are Roger and Ricky. The motel manager guesses correctly:

MOTEL MANAGER
Mr. Cho? You're in cabin seven. Well, tent seven. Here's the key, but there's no door (just a flap). Ha-ha.

The motel manager smiles, uneasy. Roger hesitates, skeptical:

ROGER
Tent?

MOTEL MANAGER
(regretfully)
I know.

In the background: Clifford enters hyperventilating with his tongue sticking out. He begins to fill up/guzzle down paper cones of water one after another from a dispenser in the corner while the motel manager continues to explain to Roger:

MOTEL MANAGER
I upgraded the electrical system Tuesday morning. Better lighting, power for the ice-machine, and a wall-mounted bug-zapper. Unfortunately, a mistake got made, and cabin seven burned to the ground. It's a tent now.

ROGER
(in disbelief)
We don't want to sleep in a tent.

MOTEL MANAGER
(soothing)
Of course, I understand. May I say: I think you'll find it very comfortable.
(distracted)
Is the young gentleman in distress?

The motel manager points. Clifford is now kneeling below the water dispenser, drinking directly from its spigot. J.J. waits in the doorway nearby:

J.J.
He's thirsty.

MOTEL MANAGER
Of course, I understand.
(to Roger)
Juice preference, please. Apple, orange, or tomato?

Just outside: an arcade of fifteen vending machines (sodas, candy, snacks, coffee, milk, fruit, toiletries, nylon stockings). The posse of cowboys and ranch hands loiters as Montana fights with the cigarette machine, banging it with his fists, then kicking it. The motel manager pokes his head out the window and shouts, anxious:

MOTEL MANAGER
Excuse me, sir?

MONTANA
(frustrated)
This bucket of nuts just stole my quarter.

MOTEL MANAGER
(apologetic)
I beg your pardon.

The motel manager ducks back inside. All the vending machines light up at once and begin to hum. Montana tries the machine again and receives his pack of cigarettes.

Camera now makes its way through the neat, little compound of freshly painted bungalows and small palm trees; past a cabin which has incinerated completely to a cinder except for its bathtub; past an immediately adjacent canvas tent; past a communal shower where a woman in a bathrobe and slippers is waiting outside clutching a folded towel and a bar of soap; and finally to Augie and his family, who have arranged themselves, seated on suitcases, stumps, and footstools, outside the open door of a bungalow marked “Cabin #10.” An unseen figure inside operates a vacuum cleaner.

In his hands, Augie holds: a green and yellow Tupperware salad bowl, sealed. In the background: a gardener/handyman tends to a flower bed; the breeze rustles linens hanging from a clothesline; a yipping terrier chases a thrown stick; big band music plays softly from a radio. Augie says, pained, as camera comes to a stop:

AUGIE
And, to put it bluntly, after all the surgeries, therapies, and interventions, after two years of struggling and suffering: she succumbed to her illnesses.

Woodrow and his sisters are immobile and thunderstruck. Tears run down Augie's cheeks.

AUGIE
I'm sorry. I didn't know how to tell you then. I couldn't figure out how to tell you later. I didn't know what to do. The time was never right.

Silence. Woodrow finally asks:

WOODROW
You're saying our mother died three weeks ago?

AUGIE
Yes.

The three girls begin to cry continuously at a low decibel from this point through the end of the scene. Andromeda asks, sobbing:

ANDROMEDA
When is she coming back?

AUGIE
(excruciatingly)
She's <u>not</u> coming back. Let's say she's in heaven, which doesn't exist for me, of course -- but you're Episcopalian.

Augie hugs the family together. They sit for a minute, absorbing the situation. Augie says to Woodrow:

AUGIE
Did you know? Already.

WOODROW
I think so.

Augie nods. He says softly:

AUGIE
She'd been away so long.
(pause)
We're going to be OK. Your grandfather's on his way. We're going to stay with him for -- a period of time which has yet to be determined how long it's going to be.

Woodrow points at the bowl. Augie nods again, holding back tears as he says with the slightest twinkle at the absurdity of it:

AUGIE
Yes. She's in the Tupperware.

Pause. Augie suddenly clarifies for the girls, who look slightly confused:

AUGIE
Cremated.

Woodrow peels open a corner of the top of the bowl and peers inside. He reseals it. Pandora asks, weeping:

PANDORA
Are we orphans now?

AUGIE
(pause)
No, because I'm still alive.

Pandora nods. Augie reaches into the past:

AUGIE
When my father died, my mother told me, "He's in the stars." I told her, "The closest star other than that one --"
(pointing to the sun)
"-- is four and half light years away with a surface temperature over 5000 degrees centigrade. He's not in the stars," I said. "He's in the ground." She thought it would comfort me. (She was an atheist.) The other thing she said which is incorrect: "Time heals all wounds." No. Maybe it can be a Band-Aid. Your concept of time is completely distorted, though. I don't think any of you except Woodrow even understands what fifteen minutes means.

PANDORA
(whimpering)
Fifteen minutes is sixty-two hundred hours.

AUGIE
Exactly. That's not your fault. I definitely handled this wrong, by the way -- but handling it right wouldn't've helped, either.

Woodrow and his sisters gaze into space. Augie says finally, hopeful:

AUGIE
If you could have anything in the world to eat right now: what would it be?

INT. LUNCHEONETTE. DAY

The three sisters sit at the counter eating banana splits, eyes red from crying. Woodrow sips a vanilla milkshake with a striped straw. Augie sadly tamps his pipe. In the background, outside the window: the posse of cowboys and ranch hands rush into view and hurriedly grab up baggage left behind for them on the tarmac (including guitar/banjo/bass fiddle cases) and race scrambling after the bus; but it drives away without them. Then: the Chevy pursued by the state trooper races by again in the opposite direction, dragging its muffler. (A pair of motorcycle police have now joined the chase.) The sounds of the engines and popping gunshots diminish. Pause.

Augie looks down the length of the diner. At the far end: Midge and Dinah are finishing a late breakfast. (The driver/bodyguard seated alone in a corner, works on a crossword puzzle.) Augie watches for a moment, then winds his camera and takes a picture. Midge looks to Augie directly after the shutter clicks. She frowns. She says loudly across the room with food in her mouth:

MIDGE
You took a picture of me.

Woodrow and Dinah look up. Augie answers:

AUGIE
Uh-huh.

MIDGE
Why?

AUGIE
(shrugs)
I'm a photographer.

MIDGE
You didn't ask permission.

AUGIE
I never ask permission.

MIDGE
Why not?

AUGIE
Because I work in trenches, battlefields, and combat zones.

MIDGE
(surprised)
Really?

AUGIE
Uh-huh.

MIDGE
(intrigued)
You mean you're a war photographer.

AUGIE
(vaguely)
Mostly. Sometimes I cover sporting events. My name is Augie Steenbeck.

Long pause. Woodrow and Dinah meet eyes. Woodrow quickly returns to his milkshake. Dinah watches him coolly. Midge presses on:

MIDGE
What are you going to do with it? That picture.

Augie considers this. He says theoretically:

AUGIE
If it's any good, I guess I'll try to sell it to a magazine, now that you mention it. "Midge Campbell Eating a Waffle."

MIDGE
Make me a print first. To approve.

AUGIE
Uh-huh.

Dinah raises her hand. Midge looks at her.

MIDGE
This is Dinah.

AUGIE
(pause)
This is Woodrow.

DINAH
I have a question.

AUGIE
(pause)
Uh-huh.

DINAH
Have _you_ ever been shot? With bullets.

Midge looks at her daughter and raises an eyebrow. Augie says, slightly reluctant:

AUGIE
Once or twice. Just grazed.

WOODROW
He got shrapneled in the back of the head, too.
(to Augie)
Show her.

Augie sighs. He twists, and Woodrow points to a bald dot above the nape of Augie's neck. Dinah nods, interested. Midge turns back to her waffles -- but says pointedly (without looking):

MIDGE
I don't say I forgive you yet, by the way.

EXT. METEOR CRATER. DAY

A congregation has assembled at the bottom/center of the impact crater below the observatory. The audience of parents, guardians, schoolchildren, and military personnel sits in folding chairs in front of a make-shift stage and dais. A banner decorated with stars, comets, and rockets reads:

ASTEROID DAY 1955
Sponsored by
the United States Military-science
Research and Experimentation Division
& the LARKINGS Foundation
"For a Powerful America"

A uniformed aide-de-camp stands next to an American flag waving on a short flagpole. A business executive in a dark suit (with a badge on the lapel: "LARKINGS Corp.") sits discreetly in the background. Woodrow, Dinah, Clifford, Roger, and Shelly wait on display in an uneasy row behind a table arranged with five neat red-white-and-blue velvet boxes. Augie is in the audience with the girls who are now made-up as witches and goblins with plastic fangs and claws. A cameraman films the proceedings in 16mm from a tripod on a rickety scaffolding tower.

(NOTE: from this scene forward most of the visiting parents, students, judges, et al. wear tags displaying their full names and the stars/comets/rockets motif.)

At a lectern also decorated with the stars/comets/rockets motif stands: a tall, square-jawed, broad-shouldered, immaculately pressed and polished five-star officer in his mid-fifties. He is General Gibson. His voice reverberates over a P.A. speaker:

GENERAL GIBSON
Welcome! From the United States Military-science Research and Experimentation Division (in conjunction with the Larkings Foundation). We salute you.

Reserved applause as General Gibson salutes in various directions. He refers to his notes (typewritten, orderly) and begins:

GENERAL GIBSON
Each year we celebrate "Asteroid Day," commemorating September 23, 3007 B.C. when the Arid Plains meteorite made earth-impact.

General Gibson motions to the small, spherical rock within the rebar cage at the center of the crater.

GENERAL GIBSON
The itinerary for this three-day celebration includes a tour of the newly refurbished observatory with Dr. Hickenlooper and her staff --

General Gibson motions to a woman (age: fifty) dressed in red plaid trousers, climbing boots, and a belted leather jacket. She is Dr. Hickenlooper. Her younger assistant wears a white lab coat.

GENERAL GIBSON
-- a picnic supper of chili and frankfurters with evening fireworks display --

General Gibson motions to the waitress, cashier, and cook seated together in the audience; and, next to them, the mechanic who now wears a badge: "Pyrotechnics Expert."

GENERAL GIBSON
-- the viewing of the Astronomical Ellipses at its peak (just before midnight tonight) --

General Gibson looks up at the sky. He looks back down to the audience.

GENERAL GIBSON
-- and finally, the awarding of the annual Hickenlooper Scholarship after Monday's banquet lunch.

General Gibson motions to the aide-de-camp, who holds up: a giant-sized cashier's check in the amount of $5,000 made out to "New Hickenlooper Scholar." He looks briefly to the five teenagers and motions to the boxes on the table.

GENERAL GIBSON
I'll start by presenting the commemorative medals -- but, first, I'll do my speech, first (which you'll also receive in a folio edition as a souvenir).

During the following recitation, General Gibson gives a carefully rehearsed performance, modulating pace, volume, and emphasis for dramatic effect:

GENERAL GIBSON
"Chapter one: I walked to school eighteen miles each morning, milked the goats, plucked the chickens, played hooky, caught fireflies, went skinny-dipping in the watering hole, said my prayers every night, and got whipped with a maple switch twice a week. That was life. Chapter two: my father went off to fight in the war to end all wars (it didn't), and what-was-left-of-him came back in a pine box with a flag on top. End of chapter two. Next: I went to officer school and twenty years passed at the speed of a dream. A wife, a son, a daughter, a poodle. Chapter three: another war. Arms and legs blown off like popcorn. Eyeballs gouged out, figuratively and literally. The men put on shows under the palm fronds dressed as women in hula skirts. That was life. In the meantime, somebody else's story: a man thinks up a number, divides it by a trillion, plugs it into the square root of the circumference of the earth multiplied by the speed of a splitting atom -- and *voila!* Progress. I'm not a scientist. <u>You</u> are. End of chapter three. Junior Stargazers and Space Cadets --"

General Gibson motions to the schoolchildren, seated with June and the chaperones.

GENERAL GIBSON
"-- we watch, transfixed, as you enter into uncharted territories of the brains and spirit. If you wanted to live a nice, quiet, peaceful life: you picked the
(more)

GENERAL GIBSON (cont'd)
wrong time to get born." That's my speech.

Silence. Suddenly: enthusiastic (if slightly puzzled) applause from the whole group.

GENERAL GIBSON
Be notified: you are each the guardian of your own safety. Maintain alert caution throughout the following demonstrations.

MONTAGE:

First: Ricky (in safety helmet, gloves, and boots) manipulates the controls of a roaring jet-pack as he hovers twenty feet above the cowering audience, blasting them with dust and dirt. His father, grimacing on the ground, clings to the end of a rope tether, struggling to prevent his son from rocketing up higher into the sky.

GENERAL GIBSON (V.O.)
To Ricky Cho, for his work in the field of Aeronautical Induction:

General Gibson pops open one of the velvet boxes and presents the contents to Ricky as he announces his prize:

GENERAL GIBSON
"The Collapsing Star Ribbon of Success."

Next: a heavy, clay plate catapults into the air as Clifford hoists a metallic-and-plastic electromagnetic death-ray up to his shoulder and pulls the trigger, silently zapping the plate into a shower of glowing dots which linger in space, sizzling, then pop away like electric soap bubbles.

GENERAL GIBSON (V.O.)
To Clifford Kellogg, for his work in the study of Particle Disintegration:

General Gibson presents/announces Clifford's prize:

GENERAL GIBSON
"The Black Hole Badge of Triumph."

Next: faces crowd all around a terracotta pot filled with black soil inside a glass incubation box.

GENERAL GIBSON (V.O.)
To Dinah Campbell, for her work in the area of Botanical Acceleration:

Dinah turns a dial. A quartet of coiled tubes at the upper corners of the box begin to hum and vibrate, and a green stem pokes up out of the dirt, uncurls, grows, and finally delivers a perfect geranium blossom -- which almost immediately withers and sheds its petals.

DINAH
It's fueled by cosmic radiation instead of sunlight. Unfortunately, it makes vegetables toxic.

General Gibson presents/announces Dinah's prize:

GENERAL GIBSON (V.O.)
"The Red Giant Sash of Honor."

Next: Shelly stands next to a large periodic table on a stand as she displays a hunk of doughy, grey paste in a mason jar.

GENERAL GIBSON (V.O.)
To Shelly Borden, for her work in the realm of Mineral Fabrication:

Shelly opens the jar, shakes the hunk of paste into her hand, and squishes it slightly. She politely announces:

SHELLY
I synthesized an extraterrestrial element. It's going to be added to the periodic table next year.

General Gibson presents/announces Shelly's prize:

GENERAL GIBSON
"The Distant Nebula Laurel Crown."

Next: Woodrow glances now and then to the sky as he carefully adjusts the angles of hinged lenses and mirrors on a doughnut-shaped erection of beams, posts, and braces.

GENERAL GIBSON (V.O.)
To Woodrow Steenbeck, for his work in the sphere of Astronomical Imaging:

Woodrow steps back and double-checks a list in his notebook. He clicks a switch, illuminating a circle of light bulbs. A hologram of the moon the size of a beach ball appears at the center of the device, rotating slowly, pocked with crisply-rendered craters.

General Gibson presents/announces Woodrow's prize:

GENERAL GIBSON
"The White Dwarf Medal of Achievement."

Not yet finished: Woodrow drops a small, glass slide into a slot, casting the image of an American flag onto the surface of the hologram-moon. He points up. Everyone looks. In the clear, afternoon sky: the American flag appears in full color on the surface of the actual moon itself. A collective gasp from the audience. Spontaneous, giddy applause. Woodrow says calmly:

WOODROW
It may have applications in the development of interstellar advertising.

Finally: the five teenagers (now wearing their various pins, medals, sashes, etc.) bow and smile, politely accepting an enthusiastic ovation.

INT. OBSERVATORY. DAY

A classroom separated by glass-partition-walls from the adjacent laboratory offices and dormitory chambers. Children/teenagers sit in school desks. Adults (parents, teachers, military) stand crowded around the edges of the room. Outside: the field of spinning radio telescopes. Dr. Hickenlooper, at a table in front, concludes:

DR. HICKENLOOPER
Our little tour ends here. Thank you for your attention -- and thank you to the Larkings Foundation for their generous funding.

The audience filters their way out the door. Woodrow lingers next to Dr. Hickenlooper as she puts on lipstick in a compact mirror. He points to a small display on the terrace outside: a scoreboard decorated with varicolored light-bulbs and blinking panels. It emits a repetitive combination of electronic noises.

WOODROW
What do those pulses indicate?

DR. HICKENLOOPER
(zipping her handbag)
What? Oh, the beeps and blips. We don't know. Indecipherable radio emissions from outer space. Probably a red herring.

WOODROW
(pause)
Does it change? Ever.

DR. HICKENLOOPER
Not to my knowledge.

WOODROW
It's a date. Maybe.

Dr. Hickenlooper squints at the display. She nods slowly.

DR. HICKENLOOPER
It's a date? Maybe.

WOODROW
On the galactic calendar.

DR. HICKENLOOPER
(hollering)
Mary!

Dr. Hickenlooper's assistant appears at her side, curious. Dr. Hickenlooper nods at Woodrow as she speculates:

DR. HICKENLOOPER
We think it's a date on the galactic calendar.

ASSISTANT
(surprised)
Wow!

Woodrow checks his watch. He frowns.

WOODROW
Is it always today?

Dr. Hickenlooper checks her own watch. She looks at Woodrow, puzzled/impressed.

EXT. MOTEL GARDEN. EVENING

Strung lights in the shapes of little planets festoon the palm trees. The juke box (now outdoors) plays a lush/romantic orchestral tune. The luncheonette waitress and cook serve from pots and trays (chili, hot dogs, potato chips and potato salad, pickles, stacks of white bread) at a buffet on the edge of an arrangement of white-papered picnic tables which seat festive groups in mid-supper: the five teenagers; the parents/guardians; the military personnel; the school group; Dr. Hickenlooper and her assistant; the posse of cowboys and ranch hands who missed the bus.

Table #1: the freckled boy says grace for his classmates, teacher, and chaperones:

FRECKLED BOY
We thank Thee for the ketchup, and we thank Thee for the mustard. We thank Thee for the relish, and we thank Thee for the onions. We thank Thee for the --

JUNE
(suddenly)
Head count!

The children/chaperones hesitate, looking at each other, uncertain. They chirp their numbers once again -- but there is a silence after "six." June frowns. She says, anxious:

JUNE
Where's Dwight?

Table #2: J.J., Roger, and Sandy engage in a slightly combative debate:

J.J.
Less than zero-point-zero-zero-zero-zero-zero-zero percent chance exists of extraterrestrial life in the entire universe. It's a scientific fact. Other than space bugs and microscopic worms.

ROGER
I assertively disagree.

SANDY
So do I. It's <u>not</u> a scientific fact.

ROGER
It's not even a number.

SANDY
Pass the pickles, please.

The motel manager interjects as he lights sparklers and passes them to his guests:

MOTEL MANAGER
How's the chili?

J.J.
(without looking up)
Fine.

MOTEL MANAGER
Thank you.

J.J.
Once you add the hot sauce.

ROGER
(passing the pickles)
Consider the constants: endless space and immeasurable time. The likelihood is increased by a factor of infinity.

J.J.
(distracted)
Where'd you get that?

The driver/bodyguard, listening nearby, sips a dry martini from an undersized glass. The motel manager chimes in warmly:

MOTEL MANAGER
The cantina machine.

Roger and Sandy perk up considerably. Augie and Midge, opposite each other at the head and foot of the table, conduct a separate/simultaneous conversation:

AUGIE
Can you see anything? With those on your face.

Midge points to her dark sunglasses ("These?"), then removes them -- revealing a severe black-eye/shiner with purple, pink, and yellow highlights. Augie looks surprised but responds with clinical stoicism:

AUGIE
Gadzooks. What'd you do to deserve that?

MIDGE
Nothing.

AUGIE
Who hit you?

MIDGE
Nobody.

Midge licks her finger and rubs the bruise. It smudges slightly. Augie squints. Midge explains:

MIDGE
It's greasepaint. To feel like my character. It's there on purpose.

AUGIE
(intrigued/confused)
Oh.

Augie contemplates this for a moment. He says finally:

AUGIE
How does she get a black eye? In the story.

MIDGE
She doesn't. In the story. It's on the inside.

Table #3: General Gibson and the business executive review a sheaf of documents:

EXECUTIVE
The Larkings Foundation claims permanent, incontestable rights to all patents or inventions derived from any and every submission, without exception.

GENERAL GIBSON
Not for teenagers. (Read the fine print.) The projects all belong to Uncle Sam.

Table #4 ("Reserved for Junior Stargazer Honorees"): Clifford does a yo-yo trick for Dinah, Ricky, and Shelly.

CLIFFORD
I call it: "Triple Orbit and Return without Burning up in the Atmosphere."

Clifford swirls the yo-yo three times into the air, then whips it back quickly. He watches to see how impressed the others are. (Hard to judge.) Dinah looks away -- then says suddenly to an off-screen character:

DINAH
Why are you sitting there all by yourself?

At a remove of approximately twenty feet: Woodrow is perched on a metal camper's ice chest with his dinner plate in his lap. He looks around in all directions to determine if he is the person actually being addressed.

DINAH
Are you shy?

WOODROW
(long pause)
I'm a late bloomer. So I've been told (by my parents).

CLIFFORD
(bluntly)
Are you intimidated by us?

WOODROW
(short pause)
No.

CLIFFORD
Let's do a personality test. (What's your name, again?)

WOODROW
(hesitates)
Woodrow L. Steenbeck.

RICKY
What's the "L" for?

WOODROW
Lindbergh.

CLIFFORD
Everybody: look at Woodrow.

Dinah, Clifford, Ricky, and Shelly all stare intently at Woodrow. Woodrow turns bright red, but meets their eyes. Clifford nods wisely.

CLIFFORD
I agree: shy, but not intimidated.

RICKY
Move over here, Woodrow.

Ricky nods to a vacant seat at the picnic table. Woodrow reluctantly transports himself and his dinner. (In the background, Clifford climbs an ivied trellis.) Dinah points at Woodrow's hat as he sits:

DINAH
"Brainiac." It sort of goes without saying, doesn't it? Everybody already knows we're abnormally intelligent.

WOODROW
(hesitates)
That's true. My mother made it for me. It's supposed to be funny (according to her sense of humor) -- but it's not as hilarious as it was originally.

DINAH
How come?

WOODROW
Because she was alive then. Now she's dead.

DINAH
Oh.

WOODROW
(oddly)
Ha-ha.

Ricky and Shelly look away/down, nod and murmur, uncomfortable. Dinah asks Woodrow:

DINAH
What was she like?

Woodrow thinks for a moment. Dinah, Ricky, and Shelly stare intently at him again. They suddenly look concerned. Woodrow, as before, has turned bright red, now with puffy eyes and tears streaming down his face. He appears to be, nevertheless, still searching for an answer. Dinah, Ricky, and Shelly wait, speechless. Woodrow reaches into his pocket and takes out a photograph. He shows it.

WOODROW
Like this.

INSERT:

A snapshot of a dazzling, dark-eyed, thirty-year-old brunette in a one-piece bathing suit laughing, exuberant, as she bathes in an inflatable swimming pool on a downtown fire-escape.

Dinah studies the picture. She says, solemn:

DINAH
When'd you lose her?

WOODROW
(hesitates)
Officially? This morning (but I think I already knew).

Dinah looks shocked/confused. Clifford's voice interrupts, calling from off-screen:

CLIFFORD (O.S.)
Howdy!

Woodrow, Dinah, Ricky, and Shelly look all around -- then up: Clifford has climbed onto the roof of the closest bungalow where he stands, hands on hips, legs apart, casually heroic. Shelly frowns.

SHELLY
What are you doing up there?

CLIFFORD
(shrugs)
Just enjoying the night air.

Woodrow, Dinah, Ricky, and Shelly watch Clifford briefly, faintly annoyed. Clifford continues:

CLIFFORD
You dare me?

SHELLY
(blankly)
Dare you what?

CLIFFORD
To jump off this bungalow. It's an experiment.

RICKY

No.

Clifford leaps off the rooftop (flailing deliberately as he aims for a patch of thick grass which he partially misses) and bangs into a garbage can which spills orange peels, soups cans, processed meat tins, etc. He stands up, limping but pleased, and picks grass off his skin. Woodrow (who, looking at his watch, appears to have timed the descent) says, aside:

WOODROW

I love gravity. It might be my favorite law of physics, at the moment.

INSERT:

A vending machine labeled "Martini with Twist." In a window on the front of the unit: a lemon on a little spool spins while an automated paring knife curls free a sliver of peel -- which drops down to garnish a clear liquid in a glass cup.

EXT. MOTEL OFFICE. EVENING

The motel manager passes the martini to J.J., who is just finishing a previous cup. Roger's and Sandy's are half-full/half-empty.

J.J.

Be that as it may, I strongly question whether your daughter's Silly-Putty resembles anything from outer space.

SANDY

It's not Silly-Putty.

J.J.

I'm sorry, but I doubt it.

SANDY

It's called S'morestozium.

J.J. clinks Sandy's glass and takes a sip. He is impressed.

J.J.

This is excellent.

MOTEL MANAGER

(modest but proud)

Thank you. It's really all the machine's doing.

SANDY

What the devil do you know about Astrogeology, anyway, J.J. (whatever that stands for)?

MOTEL MANAGER
I just maintain the workings.

SANDY
Shelly's thesis is supported by --

ROGER
(interrupting)
"Flimsy, outdated evidence."

SANDY
(slightly taken aback)
I beg your pardon?

ROGER
Not in my opinion. I liked the Silly-Putty (or S'morestozium, in fact). I'm quoting what he said.

Roger points at J.J. The motel manager laughs suddenly. J.J. frowns. He responds to Roger:

J.J.
Your son's project very well might've killed us all today, by the way.

SANDY
(gently icy)
Coming from the family that brought us the electromagnetic death-ray.

J.J.
(obviously)
It's a weapon. Of course, it's lethal.

SANDY
(twizzling her drink)
So you admit it!

J.J.
Not to mention Brainiac's flag. Is he trying to provoke World War III?

ROGER
The jet propulsion belt is eminently safe. I'd allow an eight-year-old boy to operate it. In fact, I did (Ricky's cousin Chip), and he broke the solo-flight altitude record.

MOTEL MANAGER
(pause)
They're strange aren't they? Your children. Compared to normal people.

On this point: J.J., Sandy, and Roger all sharply agree (and are even slightly emotional contemplating the subject).

EXT. MOTEL CABIN #7. EVENING

Between the burned ruin and the canvas tent: the five teenagers sit together in a circle on the ground (under a pink oleander, near a humming air conditioning unit). Dinah rapidly explains the rules of a game:

DINAH
After that, the second person says the name the first one said and adds another; then the third person says both plus a new name; then the next person keeps going and so on in a circle. It's a memory game. Get it?

RICKY
I think so.

DINAH
I'll start. Cleopatra.

RICKY
(pause)
Cleopatra, Jagadish Chandra Bose. Like that?

Dinah nods. The five teenagers adjust and re-situate themselves, physically and mentally. Shelly picks up where Ricky left off:

SHELLY
Cleopatra, Jagadish Chandra Bose, Antonie van Leeuwenhoek.

CLIFFORD
(eagerly)
Cleopatra, Jagadish Chandra Bose, Antonie van Leeuwenhoek -- Paracelsus.

Clifford raises an eyebrow. Woodrow points to each player as he recalls his/her name:

WOODROW
Cleopatra, Jagadish Chandra Bose, Antonie van Leeuwenhoek, Paracelsus --
(pointing to himself)
Kurt Gödel.

A murmur of appreciation. Camera now pans from one player to the next as Dinah lists:

DINAH
Cleopatra, Jagadish Chandra Bose, Antonie van Leeuwenhoek, Paracelsus, Kurt Gödel --
(pause)
William Bragg.

Clifford and Ricky interject immediately:

CLIFFORD
Which one?

RICKY
There's two.

Dinah quickly clarifies:

DINAH
William <u>Henry</u> Bragg.

A murmur of acceptance. Exchanged looks as the group prepares for the next round. Ricky pauses, then recites speedily:

RICKY
Cleopatra, Jagadish Chandra Bose, Antonie van --

Ricky hesitates an instant. Everyone chimes in just as he remembers:

RICKY
Leeuwenhoek.

OTHERS
Leeuwenhoek.

RICKY
(continuing)
Paracelsus, Kurt Gödel, William Henry Bragg.

Ricky nods, satisfied. He says suddenly (as Dinah chimes in):

RICKY
Lord Kelvin.

DINAH
Add the new one.

SHELLY
(immediately)
Cleopatra, Jagadish Chandra Bose, Antonie van Leeuwenhoek, Paracelsus, Kurt Gödel, William Henry Bragg, Lord Kelvin --

Pause. Shelly looks to Dinah and says, embarrassed/excited:

SHELLY
-- Midge Campbell. (Can I say her?)

DINAH
(impassive)
As long as she's a real person. You can say anybody you like.

CLIFFORD
Cleopatra, Jagadish Chandra Bose --

DINAH
Including my mother.

SHELLY
She's my idol.

CLIFFORD
(bristling)
My turn. Jagadish Chandra Bose, Antonie van Leeuwenhoek, Paracelsus, Kurt Gödel, William Bragg (the father), Lord Kelvin (the mathematical physicist), Midge Campbell (your mother) --
(pleasantly)
-- Konstantin Tsiolkovsky (the rocket scientist).

A murmur of annoyance. Ricky says, uncertain:

RICKY
I don't know if this game works with us. Brainiacs, I mean. I think it might go on forever.

SHELLY
I don't mind. In my school, nobody'd play this game with me in a million years -- plus the names'd be too obvious.

CLIFFORD
I know my next one. Diophantus.

A murmur of further annoyance. Dinah proposes to Woodrow:

DINAH
Try it backwards, Brainiac. Say the new one first.

Woodrow pauses. He points to himself first:

WOODROW
Hōjō Tokiyuki.

Woodrow then goes carefully backwards through the group:

WOODROW
Konstantin Tsiolkovsky, Midge Campbell, Lord Kelvin, William Henry Bragg, Kurt
(more)

WOODROW (cont'd)
Gödel, Paracelsus, Antonie van Leeuwenhoek, Jagadish Chandra Bose --

Woodrow stops at Dinah. Pause.

WOODROW
Cleopatra.

EXT. DESERT. EVENING

Outside the fence at the rear the motel: the posse of cowboys and ranch hands have pitched camp for the night (an open fire, a circle of sleeping bags, saddles and tack, a strummed banjo) fifty yards into the desert. They perch on rocks and rucksacks, smoking cigarettes and sipping at bottles of beer. They watch as June swings one leg then another over the fence, agile, and strides out toward them. She arrives, glaring.

JUNE
Put out that cigarette, Dwight.

One of June's pupils (a boy with a cowlick) puffs a last puff at a cigarette butt. He darts it into the fire.

JUNE
You men should be ashamed of yourselves.

The cowboys and ranch hands exchange looks: puzzled, amused, embarrassed. June presses the question:

JUNE
<u>Are</u> you?

Montana stands up. He interjects, courtly and (perhaps) honest:

MONTANA
Yes, ma'am. We didn't give him that.

MONTANA
(clarifying)
That cigarette.

JUNE
(coolly)
Didn't you?

MONTANA
No, ma'am. He just must've got it his own self.

Montana smiles/laughs. June looks to the boy. The boy shrugs. June and Montana study each other briefly. June says (less cool):

JUNE
I almost believe you.
(to the boy)
Let's go.

The boy reluctantly drags himself to his feet, nodding to the men as they murmur polite goodbyes. Montana tips his hat to June. June rolls her eyes. She takes the boy by the hand and starts briskly back toward the fence.

INT. MOTEL CABINS #9/10. EVENING

Cabin #9: Midge paces back and forth in the open window of her bathroom while she reads aloud from a screenplay, rehearsing herself (half off-book):

MIDGE
"Was I ever there? Was I _ever_ there? Was I ever _there_? Did you actually --"

Cabin #10: a roller-blind zings open in another bathroom window (directly opposite, just across a narrow driveway). Inside, Augie has set up a darkroom with blankets and strings, a red lamp and enlarger, etc. He looks out, wiggling and fanning a damp print. Midge pauses and sees him.

MIDGE
Memorizing my lines.

AUGIE
Uh-huh.

Augie reverses the photograph to show: "Midge Campbell Eating a Waffle." Beautifully lit, perfectly natural, wildly flattering. Pause.

MIDGE
Approved.

Augie turns away to hang the print (next to his photo of the atomic explosion) to dry with clothespins. Midge sits down inside her window. Augie sits down inside his.

MIDGE
I do a nude scene. Want to see it?

Silence. Augie suddenly flickers alert:

AUGIE
Did I say, "Yes?"

MIDGE
You didn't say anything.

AUGIE
I meant, "Yes." My mouth didn't speak.

MIDGE
It's a monologue. It starts when I turn off the shower.

Midge stands up. She walks into the bathroom, turns on the shower, takes off her clothes, steps into the bathtub, closes the curtain, and stands under the running water for five seconds. She turns off the shower. She steps back out. She wraps herself in a towel. Backlit in the bathroom doorway, she recites:

MIDGE
"When you first picked me out of the secretarial pool, I had a hundred and eleven dollars in my bank account. I lived alone with a cat and a parakeet in a one-room dishwater flat. I sold the DeSoto to lend you the down-payment for my engagement ring. It was spring... I'm not sore: I know you're a good man. I'm not sorry: I never deceived you. Remember me as a blur in the rearview mirror. Was I ever there? Did you <u>actually</u> see me? I can't even see myself anymore -- but here I am.

Midge unwraps her towel, dangles it slowly, then lets it slip to the floor. She stares at Augie. Augie stares back, serenely frozen. Midge says, hopeful/resigned/determined:

MIDGE
Let's get divorced."

Silence. Midge says eventually:

MIDGE
It'll be done tastefully, of course. We cut to the back of my legs when the towel falls down.

AUGIE
(pause)
Sometimes they do a stunt-double.

MIDGE
(undecided)
Sometimes. I don't know if I like beards, by the way.

Augie nods. He puts his pipe into his mouth and lights it. Midge flips two switches on the wall: turning off the overhead bathroom light and turning on a pair of dressing-table mirror-tubes, which illuminate her softly in blue-ish. She reaches for a *peignoir* -- but Augie interrupts (reacting to the entire vignette):

AUGIE
Oh. Can I take another picture? Not for publication.

MIDGE
(long pause)
I thought you never ask permission.

Augie shrugs. Midge holds still (for a very long exposure) as Augie snaps the photograph. Midge puts on her dressing gown and returns to her window-seat. She confides to Augie:

MIDGE
I prefer to play abused, tragic alcoholics, and one day I'll probably be discovered lifeless in an overflowing bathtub with an empty bottle of sleeping pills spilled all over the floor -- but the sad thing is: I'm actually a very gifted comedienne.

AUGIE
(genuinely)
That's true.

MIDGE
Are you married?

AUGIE
I'm a widower -- but don't tell my kids.

MIDGE
Why not? I mean: I wasn't going to. I'm sorry.

AUGIE
Thank you. They do know, by the way -- but just barely.

EXT. MOTEL CABIN #10. EVENING

In an alley behind the cabin: Andromeda, Pandora, and Cassiopeia crouch on their knees as they dig a small hole in the ground with a fork, a spoon, and a popsicle stick. The Tupperware salad bowl waits beside them. In the background: a mint-green Cadillac Eldorado convertible curls from the highway, rolls into the driveway, and stops. Pandora commands her sisters:

PANDORA
Put the potion in it.

Stanley (in golfing attire, as before) gets out of the car and slowly approaches as: Andromeda produces the previously-prepared ashtray of salt, pepper, and mustard; Pandora decants the remaining drops of a jar of vinegar into the mixture; and Cassiopeia stirs it all together, then scoops out bits at a time with the popsicle stick, shoveling the potion down the hole in the ground as she invents/recites:

CASSIOPEIA
Friskity, triskity, briskity, boo; knickerty, knockerty, tockerty, too! And with this spell: Mama comes back -- alive!

The girls wait for a moment while nothing happens. Stanley pauses just behind them. Andromeda pronounces:

ANDROMEDA
God save these bones.

The girls place the bowl into the hole, throw dead flowers on top, and begin to spoon/fork dirt in after. Stanley says finally:

STANLEY
What's in the Tupperware?

The girls look up at their grandfather, startled, and stare. Stanley studies the expressions on their faces; then says, slightly heartbroken:

STANLEY
He finally told you.

The girls turn back to the gravesite. Stanley comes closer and kisses the girls on the tops of their heads, one by one. Pandora murmurs as he does this:

PANDORA
Who's this old man?

CASSIOPEIA
Poppy, I think.

STANLEY
(deeply offended)
You don't remember me?

ANDROMEDA
I remember his smell.

Stanley frowns. He sniffs at his hands and arms. He makes an official decision:

STANLEY
We're not going to abandon my daughter at a motel in the middle of the desert buried next to the communal showers.

Stanley kneels down, removes the flowers, and begins to carefully dig up the bowl. The girls, at first frozen in shock, quickly go into a frenzied panic, squealing and shrieking:

CASSIOPEIA
You're ruining the funeral!

PANDORA
He's making her go to hell!

Andromeda strikes a threatening pose and clarifies the situation, seething:

ANDROMEDA
If you torture us, we'll sacrifice you.

Stanley pauses as he is about to pull the bowl up from the dirt. He sighs.

STANLEY
I understand. Thank you for your -- clarity. I'll tell you what: we'll leave her alone in the ground until tomorrow morning. Then we'll exhume the Tupperware, bring her with us in the Cadillac, and bury her again this weekend in the backyard next to the seventh hole at Rancho Palms where I live in a beautiful house with a swimming pool. Agreed?

The girls whimper and nod. Stanley re-buries the salad bowl.

STANLEY
Let's hope a coyote doesn't dig her up in the meantime. Nothing we can do about it, anyway. Look at that.

Stanley points as a fireworks display, modest but exciting, commences in the desert just beyond the motel grounds. Stanley and the three girls watch, bereft and dazzled.

EXT. MOTEL OFFICE. EVENING

As the fireworks continue to pop: Montana retrieves a toothbrush from the toiletries vending machine, then pauses to study another machine which advertises "Deeds." He asks the motel manager, curious/suspicious:

MONTANA
What do you swap for out a'this pertickler jukebox, mister?

MOTEL MANAGER
Of course, I understand. This machine: sells land.

MONTANA
Land, you say?

MOTEL MANAGER
Yes, indeed. The properties just beyond these cottages, in fact.

The motel manager motions toward a desolate, cactus-studded flat in the near distance. Montana asks, dubious:

MONTANA
Out a' this here soder-pop machine?

MOTEL MANAGER
Yes, indeed.

MONTANA
Well, now, I ain't callin' you a liar to your face, but that sounds to me like some kind a' toadswindle.

MOTEL MANAGER
(slightly defensive)
Of course, I understand. It's not a toadswindle. You put in the money: you receive a notarized deed to the land.

MONTANA
(skeptical)
How big a spread?

MOTEL MANAGER
For $10 in quarters: approximately half a tennis court.

EXT. METEOR CRATER. NIGHT

The congregation has re-assembled, this time seated on picnic blankets. They sip and crunch a midnight snack of root beer and peanuts. Dr. Hickenlooper stands at the lectern (flanked by her assistant on one side of the dais and General Gibson on the other), uplit by a reading lamp. She begins enthusiastically over the P.A. speaker:

DR. HICKENLOOPER
Tonight you're in for a real treat. I don't know how many of you ever observed an Astronomical Ellipses before. Can we get a show-of-hands?

Only Dr. Hickenlooper herself raises her hand. She looks surprised.

DR. HICKENLOOPER

Nobody! Wow. OK, well, what you're going to see is a very simple, "dot, dot, dot": three pin-points of light inside your refracting-box, which may not sound very exciting, at first -- until you consider how those dots managed to transmit themselves across a thousand billion miles of space onto that little scrap of black cardboard. Twice every fifty-seven years, when the earth, the sun, the moon, and the galactic plane of the Milky Way all combobulate along the same angle of orbital interest, the radiant energy of three neighboring stellar systems induces a parallel ecliptic transit; thus, all but proving the hypothesis of Celestial Flirtation. The hitch, of course, is that the math doesn't work! But maybe one of you, one day, will be the genius who solves that problem.

(checking her watch)

The event will begin in thirty seconds.

Dr. Hickenlooper turns off the reading lamp. The young people and most of the adults stand up eagerly and begin to fit home-made, cardboard box and wax-paper viewing devices over their heads. The military personnel use similar but industrial-manufactured, weapons-grade versions of the apparatus (nylon and stainless-steel fittings; calibrated dials and gauges). Andromeda, Cassiopeia, and Pandora use shoeboxes. Stanley sits next to them with his own normal-sized box/device.

DR. HICKENLOOPER

Remember: if you look directly at the ellipses rather than through your refracting-box, not only will you not actually <u>see</u> the effect -- but you'll burn the dots straight into your retina, probably permanently. I know that for a fact, because they're still burned into mine from when I was eleven-going-on-twelve. That's when I realized I wanted to be an astronomer, which is another story.

(urgently)

Here we go!

Dr. Hickenlooper puts on her own viewing device.

CUT TO:

Woodrow's face inside his box. He squints. Through a tinfoil sieve on top: a beam of amber light shines neatly, diagonally, onto a black construction-paper rectangle masking-taped to the cardboard directly in front of his eyes. A small, red dot appears -- followed by a white one, then a blue -- along a perfectly-spaced, horizontal line. Woodrow says, pleased:

WOODROW
There it is.

All around the crater: "ooh's" and "ahh's" among the children, parents, and military personnel. Enchanted laughter and dazzled whispering. The breeze blows. An owl hoots. Crickets chirp. Bells ring at the railroad crossing as another freight train locomotes in the dark. Dr. Hickenlooper provides a bit of commentary, speaking into the microphone from inside her box at a whisper:

DR. HICKENLOOPER
These are just marvelously luminous colors, aren't they? Very exciting! Who doesn't see it?

FRECKLED BOY
(airily)
I don't! I just see a staple.

Dr. Hickenlooper lifts her viewing device and looks to the freckled boy. She studies him briefly as he looks up at her with the box on his head. She twists the box 180 degrees backwards. The freckled boy stiffens and yelps:

FRECKLED BOY
Yipe! It works.

Dr. Hickenlooper puts her box back on. On another/nearby picnic blanket: Midge tilts the box off her head and looks at Shelly (under her own box with her movie magazine tucked under her arm). She asks bluntly:

MIDGE
Are you Shelly?

SHELLY
(startled)
Huh? Yeah!

MIDGE
I'm your idol. What's your rank?

Shelly tilts back her box. She says, transfixed:

SHELLY
Commanding-secretary.

Shelly points to a patch on her uniform. Midge takes the magazine out of Shelly's hand and flips pages.

MIDGE
I was a Cookie Trooper, myself.

Midge finds a staged photo of herself (in a kitchen, wearing an apron, frying eggs) and autographs it. She hands back the magazine. Shelly says, awed:

SHELLY
Really? Wow! What'll they say in Squad 75?

Suddenly: the radio telescopes spinning above the crater all rotate in unison to face in a single, fixed direction. Dead silence.

CUT TO:

Woodrow's black construction-paper rectangle again. A fourth dot (green, unexpected) appears in position immediately to the right of the original three. Woodrow frowns.

WOODROW
Hm?

Woodrow tilts the box off his head and looks up.

Woodrow's mouth opens. His eyes widen. He holds his breath and stares, frozen. A faint, green glow begins to irradiate his face, slowly increasing in luminosity.

Dr. Hickenlooper, her assistant, General Gibson, the aide-de-camp, Augie, Midge, and the other gathered people begin to remove their own viewing devices and watch the sky -- agog.

From above: a green-and-neon hexagonal spacecraft exactly the diameter of the crater silently descends and hovers at an altitude of fifty feet. It twists and bounces slightly, creaking. After a moment, a fan or motor of some kind engages, whirs briefly, then shuts off again.

The group of statues below watches, stunned.

A round hatch on the underside of the spacecraft irises open. A metallic pole jolts out with a clank, extends downwards three feet, and stops. A ladder-rung folds out, buzzing, at the bottom of the pole and locks into position.

Among the watching group: hyperventilation, difficulty swallowing, a few tears. General Gibson's hand instinctively moves to the sidearm holster on his belt. He snaps off the safety.

From the hatch again: a foot (size approximately 20-AAA, red/orange, nine-toed) pokes down and cautiously tests the ladder-rung. Then: a second foot; followed by (as the pole slowly and silently extends a few feet further downward before pausing again) two extremely long, double-jointed legs; a brief, carapaced torso; spindly arms; protracted, scraggly fingers; and a pleasant, red/orange, tiny-mouthed face with large and immediately lively (even anxious) eyes.

The alien looks down at the group from its perch, hesitant. (Roger and J.J. exchange a look: "See?"/"Yes.") The alien twists a handle-grip, and the pole descends like an elevator (at first, gingerly; then quickly). When it finally stops: the end of the pole (and the alien) sways gently one foot above the ground near the center of the crater. With a little plickity-plack, a small tripod unfolds at the end of the pole, touching its three ends onto the hard-packed dirt.

The alien looks to the group -- as if awaiting permission. It steps onto the earth. Pause. It crouches and leans, reaching toward the rebar cage. Pause. It lifts off the cage like a cake-dome (weightless), sets it aside, and places its hands on the sides of the meteorite. Pause. It picks up the rock and looks all around for any objection.

Augie slowly raises his camera to his eyes. He corrects exposure and focus. The alien looks to him, adjusts its pose, and waits. Augie snaps "the picture." He lowers his camera, eyes locked with the alien, and winds the film. Woodrow looks to his father, impressed.

The alien makes a quiet sound as if clearing its throat. It tucks the meteorite under its arm and steps back onto the ladder-rung. The pole rapidly ascends/retracts all the way up and into the spacecraft. The hatch spirals shut. The green-and-neon lights flicker to a new configuration. The vessel rises straight up a thousand feet, twists one rotation in place, then cruises away at an angle high above and across the moonlit desert before vanishing into space.

Silence. Augie, at a loss, finally states the obvious:

AUGIE
The alien stole the asteroid.

No one moves.

INT. TELEVISION STUDIO. EVENING

Black and white.

The host resumes his narration, spotlit in the dark, as the lights slowly come up on a new set: a writer's study in a shingled beach house. It contains a typewriter stand; a braided rug; a pine table; wicker chairs; neatly over-stuffed bookcases; faintly homoerotic paintings of horses, steers, cowboys, ranch hands; and a whirring electric fan. Tall reeds shiver in the window before a painted theatrical background of dunes and surf at dusk. Sounds of rolling waves and seagulls.

HOST
The character of Augie Steenbeck in the imaginary tale of our production was to become famously and indelibly connected to the actor who "created" the role -- a former carpenter discovered in a bit part by the play's director, Schubert Green.

The playwright, perspiring in his Western costume, finishes clacking away at a letter and zips it out of his machine just as a middle-aged secretary enters with a rack of buttered toast on a tray.

PLAYWRIGHT
I've finished my correspondence, Analisse. Please, bring me my cocktail and my pill.

SECRETARY
(correction)
Remember, the gentleman --

PLAYWRIGHT
(horrified)
Oh, no.

SECRETARY
-- referred by Mr. Green. Has arrived --

PLAYWRIGHT
(determined)
Send him away. Put him up at the Salty Skipper (or the Lighthouse Inn) and tell him to come back in the morning --
(important:)
-- but not before eleven.

The secretary sighs. She exits, and the actor who plays Augie almost immediately enters the room. He wears a soldier's khaki uniform -- but in a stylish/relaxed fashion (contrary to regulation): cap at a tilt, necktie loose, sleeves rolled up, sweat under the armpits. The host explains:

HOST
The occasion of the first meeting between playwright and player is now (in our fanciful telling) a matter of theatrical lore and legend. Setting: late autumn,
(more)

HOST (cont'd)
late afternoon, a seaside village outside the grand metropolis.

The host exits. The playwright finally notices the actor in his study and says, startled:

PLAYWRIGHT
Oh, no, again. I beg your pardon. I'm sorry: did Miss Watson not inform you? I'm indisposed.

ACTOR/AUGIE
I know, but the ice cream would've melted.

The actor plants a large, oblong mass -- paper-wrapped, twine-bound, frayed and tattered -- onto the table with a thump. He draws a slightly frightening lock-blade hunting knife from an ankle strap and begins to hack and chop at the package. The playwright retreats a step, concerned.

PLAYWRIGHT
What's this?

ACTOR/AUGIE
(hacking/chopping)
I think it's the one you like. Gooseberry Wriggle from the Frosty Spoon on East Rotterdam. I wrapped it in sawdust, newspaper, and peanut shells.

From beneath the layers of thermal insulation: a carton of ice cream begins to emerge. The playwright quickly recognizes a gooseberry-motif on the lid. He is simultaneously deeply touched, mildly suspicious, and uncomfortable. He says, tentatively playful:

PLAYWRIGHT
You shouldn't waste your spending money on an old fool like me.

ACTOR/AUGIE
(shrugs)
They gave me ten dollars bus fare, so I bought us a half-bucket, hitch-hiked, and pocketed the change.

The actor flips the sizable blade shut, then (from a trouser pocket) unfolds a collapsible camping spoon. He lifts the carton's lid and plugs the spoon into the cream-and-purple substance. He holds out a bite to the playwright's mouth. The playwright hesitates, then leans forward and eats the spoonful of ice cream like a child. Clearly, it has survived the journey intact:

PLAYWRIGHT
Cool and delicious.

The actor and the playwright trade the spoon back and forth, two strangers eating together in silence. The playwright says eventually, politely:

PLAYWRIGHT
How long have you been in the service?

ACTOR/AUGIE
(frowns)
The service. What service? I don't know what you're talking about.

PLAYWRIGHT
(stiffening)
Well, unless I've been deliberately misinformed, I believe those stripes indicate the status of a Ranking Corporal, 2nd class.

ACTOR/AUGIE
Oh. No.
(giggles)
I'm G.I. #3 in "Bugle Boy Blows the Blues." Was, anyway. We closed tonight.

PLAYWRIGHT
(intrigued)
I see. Property of the wardrobe department.

ACTOR/AUGIE
(pause)
Not anymore.

The actor declines the return of the spoon and begins to wander around the edges of the room, studying book titles and old snapshots as the playwright continues to eat.

PLAYWRIGHT
How was it, by the way?

ACTOR/AUGIE
(distracted)
The play? It stunk. You mind if I crack open a window?

PLAYWRIGHT
Not at all. It's sweltering, isn't it?

The actor struggles briefly at the window, pressing and jabbing the rickety, wooden sash. The playwright watches him, doubtful.

PLAYWRIGHT
Even the daisies and buttercups are drooping in the --
(suddenly)
That window sticks a bit.

The actor smashes his fist through a pane, flips a latch, then (now easily) slides the window open. He looks to the playwright; both laugh out loud. Pause. The actor asks, pointed but gentle:

ACTOR/AUGIE
Why does Augie burn his hand on the Quicky-Griddle?

PLAYWRIGHT
(long pause)
Well, I don't even know, myself, to tell you the truth. I hadn't planned it that way -- he just sort of did it while I was typing. Is it too extraordinary?

ACTOR/AUGIE
(short pause)
I guess the way I read it: he was looking for an excuse why his heart was beating so fast.

PLAYWRIGHT
(enchanted)
Oh. What an interesting sentiment. I love that idea. Maybe he should say it? It's a very good line.

The actor shrugs. He shakes his head. The playwright agrees:

PLAYWRIGHT
I suppose not. Not necessary.

The playwright watches as: the actor takes down one of the playwright's freshly pressed shirts from a laundry box on a shelf; pulls out the packing-tissue and begins to stuff it under his shirt (padding for a fake belly); peels off a fake moustache and sticks it into one pocket; replaces it with a fake beard tugged out of another; rubs typewriter ink into his eyebrows; exits into a small closet and closes the door -- then reemerges with the familiar Swiss camera looped around his neck. He now speaks in Augie's quiet, regional/city accent:

ACTOR/AUGIE
"It's a fact: we're not alone. The alien stole the asteroid. 'Long-thought to be a lunar splinter fragmented from the lesser moon of the hypothetical planet Magnavox-27; now considered a rogue pygmy
(more)

ACTOR/AUGIE (cont'd)

cometette.' (According to the encyclopedia.) Obviously, she would've said something to him. I'm certain of it. Your mother, I mean. She would've gotten him to tell us the secrets of the universe or yelled at him or made him laugh. She would've had a hypothesis. You remind me of her more than ever. She wasn't shy. You'll grow out of that. (I think your sisters might be aliens, too, by the way.) When I met your mother she was only nineteen. She was smoking a cigarette/reading a paperback/taking a bath in a swimsuit on a rusty fire escape a flight and a half below my camera position. Sometimes I sometimes --

(searching)

I sometimes -- I sometimes still think I still hear her -- here --

(with a finger to his ear)

-- breathing -- in the dark.

The actor looks up at the ceiling. Long pause. When he finally looks back down, his eyes are red, his face is tear-streaked, his voice cracks:

ACTOR/AUGIE

Who knows, Woodrow? Maybe she is in the stars."

The actor sits down in one of the wicker chairs. He folds his hands in his lap -- then looks suddenly to the playwright, breaking the spell. The playwright stares. He says slowly:

PLAYWRIGHT

Normally, I'd offer my advice and suggestions, but your interpretation is so perceptive and precise -- anything you do is bound to be dramatically true. You're perfect. I don't think there's anything else to say.

Silence. The actor takes off his shirt, then his trousers and socks. The lights dim except in the window. The host re-enters frame:

HOST

Often, it is the unexpected human connections which lead to the surprises of artistic discovery.

The beach house rotates away on a turntable to reveal another new set:

INT. SLEEPING COMPARTMENT

A sleeping compartment (with sitting room and bed already made up) on an overnight passenger train. The actress who plays Midge, dressed in a silvery skirt suit and matching hat, surrounded by small suitcases, hand baggage, folded fur coat, sits with her legs tucked under her as a porter serves a bottle of beer with a chilled glass. Outside: the train accelerates through a cavernous metropolitan station (as rendered by a painted theatrical backdrop winding by on rollers). A stationmaster blowing a whistle slides by; followed by the head of a young man, twenty-two, clean cut, sprinting on the platform alongside the sleeping car. (He is the actor who plays Woodrow.) He hops a bit, trying to peek into the window, then speeds ahead, out of view. An instant later, we clear the station and enter the darkness of the tunnel that will deliver the train out of the city.

HOST
Players of the stage, a tribe of troubadours and non-conformists; they lead unconventional, sometimes dangerous, lives which nourish and elevate their artistic aspirations -- and illuminate the human condition. Next: ten weeks later, the eve of "Asteroid City's" first public preview, a drawing room onboard the Apache Plainsliner bound for the California coast.

The porter exits. The actress lights a cigarette and opens the pages of a fashion magazine. A knock on the door. The actress looks up, frowning, and waits.

ACTRESS/MIDGE
It's open.

The door swings to the wall with a clack. The sprinting young man lunges into the compartment, gasping and panting, and bangs the door shut behind him. He is dressed Ivy League, winter. He says immediately, without catching his breath:

YOUNG MAN/WOODROW
Schubert says you got to come back.

The actress stares at the young man evenly. Pause.

ACTRESS/MIDGE
If I'm so important, why isn't he here himself?

The young man shrugs, still gasping, and makes an educated guess:

YOUNG MAN/WOODROW
Probably too busy. Too busy to go chasing after you. They sent me. You know who I am?

ACTRESS/MIDGE
I think so. Understudy.

YOUNG MAN/WOODROW
Understudy. That's right. Let me just --

The young man digs into his pockets, producing various scraps of paper, ticket stubs, dollar bills, bits of lint, some of which fall onto the floor. He isolates two specific tiny, folded, creased, damp, tattered documents. He displays one in each hand.

YOUNG MAN/WOODROW
He said if you're crying, I read you this one.
(swapping pages)
That's not it. Here it is.
(swapping again)
If you're hopping mad, I read you this one.

Silence. The actress says, stony:

ACTRESS/MIDGE
Give me both.

The young man shakes his head, frazzled, and attempts to clarify the options:

YOUNG MAN/WOODROW
Not what he said. He said if you're --

ACTRESS/MIDGE
Give me both.

The young man hands the actress both documents, two hands to two hands. She reads out loud from the first one:

ACTRESS/MIDGE
"Tell her she's a stuck up, low-class snob -- but she's got no good reason to be. If she sasses you, sass her back. Tell her she's a borderline neurotic with an Achilles Heel complex."

The actress looks at the young man. He nods, confirming the message, and jams his hands into his pockets, shifting from foot to foot. The actress places the document face up on the table and moves on to the second one:

ACTRESS/MIDGE

"Tell her she relies on her beauty like a wobbly crutch. It's her deepest weakness. Tell her she's got the potential for genuine greatness -- but I say with absolute certainty: she will never achieve it."

The actress places the second document down next to the first. She looks to the young man again.

ACTRESS/MIDGE

Anything else?

The young man, nodding again, slightly less winded now, reaches inside his coat and withdraws a sealed envelope.

YOUNG MAN/WOODROW

Uh-huh. He said if you're cool and collected (which I think is what I think you seem to be), then that means you probably really don't want to come back, and I got to give you this.

The young man holds out the envelope. The actress, cool and collected, does not move.

ACTRESS/MIDGE

Read it.

YOUNG MAN/WOODROW

(shaking his head again)

Not what he said. He said this one's private. Just the two of you. He said --

The young man swallows and gives up. He opens the envelope and reads, start to finish:

YOUNG MAN/WOODROW

"Dear Kim, I'm sorry I shouted and called you a spoiled bitch and a minor talent (and broke your glasses and threw them out the window). Given that I have always considered you to be the most consummately gifted living actress and a person of great intelligence and character, these statements (and actions) do not accurately reflect my true feelings. Yes, I may be a 'manipulative snake', as you once characterized me behind my back (you see, I do have my sources) -- but I love you like a sister, other than that one time in the bathroom the day we met which has never been

(more)

YOUNG MAN/WOODROW (cont'd)
repeated, as we both know. I never meant to hurt you or insult you or offend you in any way -- only to try with the few tools I have at my disposal to do my job which is: to make it work. Forgive me. We open tomorrow night, with or without you. Without: our entire devoted company will suffer complete disaster and tragic calamity -- as will a brilliant, fragile genius named Conrad Earp. With: you will enjoy the triumph of your career, which does not matter in the least. All that matters is: every second of life <u>on stage</u> -- and our friendship. Your servant, your director, and (if I may) your devoted mentor. -- Schubert Green."

The sound of the train changes suddenly (loud to soft) as it exits the tunnel. A new winding/painted backdrop reveals the city, now distant, at dusk. Snowflakes flurry and telephone poles whisk by. The actress unpins her hat, removes it, and loosens her hair. She looks the young man up and down, head to toe. Silence.

ACTRESS/MIDGE
What's your name, understudy?

The young man stares, dumb. The host re-enters the frame and looks from young man to actress to camera. He raises an eyebrow.

HOST
They continued through the night as far as Ohio, then disembarked and caught the return flight arriving two hours prior to curtain. (The talented understudy immediately replaced the original "Woodrow.")

Scene to black. The host remains lit. He continues:

HOST
Schubert Green, born Shylock Grzworvszowski.

INT. THEATRE PROSCENIUM

Behind the host, the lights come up on the theatre proscenium set -- turned around to face the audience, with painted backdrop depicting the empty house: seats, boxes, balconies. A wiry, intense, shirtless man works onstage repainting a backdrop. He is the director.

HOST
Actor, immigrant, former student of the great theatrical guru Saltzburg Keitel.

The director wanders into the wings: adjusting a lamp; resewing the trim of a costume; briefly touching-up a young actor's old-age make-up.

HOST
Known for his limitless energy, his voracious enthusiasms (a well-known actress described him, sexually, as: "an animal -- specifically a rabbit"), and his long, deep, and intimate relationship with success.

The director arrives at a makeshift bedroom installation -- fake walls, folding bunk, sink basin, toaster and hot plate -- in a deep backstage corner behind crates, carts, and flats (all labeled: Property of "Asteroid City Scenic Department" and vaguely recognizable as the luncheonette). In the background, a hulking stagehand finishes stapling lace curtains along the sides of a fake window. They both survey the space.

DIRECTOR
What do you think, Lunky?

STAGEHAND
(deepest basso)
Good.

The director begins to shadow-box in the corner. Off-screen: an annoyed/perplexed woman's voice says:

POLLY (O.S.)
I'm not going to ask what the hell's going on here.

In the fake doorway: a woman in a raincoat. Black hair with bangs, bright red lipstick, late thirties. She is Polly.

HOST
His wife, Polly, left him for an All Star second baseman during the first week of rehearsals.

The stagehand stares, uneasy. The director milks it:

DIRECTOR
My living quarters.

Polly moves slowly into the room, eye-balling the stagehand as he sheepishly evaporates. She reaches into her pocket and withdraws a legal-sized envelope:

POLLY
Sign this.

The director stiffens. He takes the envelope. He opens it and studies a document. He says, overwhelmingly relieved:

DIRECTOR
It's Clark's report card.

Polly, rearranging the decor slightly (swapping a vase, shifting a chair), responds, distracted:

POLLY
Uh-huh. What'd you think it was?

DIRECTOR
I thought maybe we were already divorced.

POLLY
Oh. Not yet -- but eventually.

The director signs the document, slips it back into the envelope, and returns it.

DIRECTOR
He made the honor roll again.

Polly nods. She looks to the director with her knuckles on her hips.

POLLY
I'm staying at Diego's penthouse; Clark's at my mother's; the apartment's empty. Why don't you just go home?

DIRECTOR
(simply)
I don't think I should be alone in a building with real windows.

The director looks out through the fake window. (Outside: more crates.) He continues:

DIRECTOR
Props makes my lunches and dinners. Make-up cuts my hair and shaves me. Costumes washes my dungarees. This is where I belong. For now.

The director reaches into a box on the table and brings out a model of the stage-version of the hexagonal spacecraft. He flips it over, studying the design. Polly examines it over his shoulder.

POLLY
Much better. Did you do the green?

The director grunts. He presses a button on the model. It illuminates, dazzling. Polly looks pleased. She says gently:

POLLY
It's been a great ten years, Schubert. I don't regret a second of it. Clark still loves you. I still love you.

DIRECTOR
(pause)
But not like before.

POLLY
(pause)
But not like before.

Polly kisses the director softly on the lips and exits directly through the fake doorway. The director starts doing chin-ups from a costume rack as the host re-enters the frame:

HOST
Schubert Green lived in the scenic bay of the Tarkington Theatre for all 785 performances of "Asteroid City." Dark nights, he stayed in the Governor's Suite of the Nebraska Hotel.

Polly pokes her head back in. The director freezes mid-chin-up.

POLLY
One last note: when Midge makes her exit in Act 3, Scene V -- try having her say the line after she closes the door.

The director pictures this. He nods. He says wisely:

DIRECTOR
I will.

Polly smiles. She exits again and closes the fake door. The director stands and waits. Through the fake door, Polly says:

POLLY
Goodbye.

The director laughs/cries. Polly's diminishing footsteps echo on the cement floor. Lights to black.

EXT. HIGHWAY. DAY

Widescreen/color.

A reinforced military barricade encircles and isolates the entire town. Signs on roadblocks read:

Strict Quarantine!
Do Not Enter (or Exit)
by order of
the United States Military-science
Research and Experimentation Division

Armed guards occupy security-posts on low scaffoldings at frequent intervals along the perimeter. A fleet of parked jeeps and troop transports provide additional fortification. Civilian vehicles in a queue on the highway wait to U-turn, one by one, as soldiers direct them to alternate routes.

INT. OBSERVATORY. DAY

The classroom. The school desks now seat military officers, technicians, and scientific advisors (including the business executive). Soldiers stand in the corners with rifles shouldered/sidearms holstered. A door opens. General Gibson strides into the room followed by his aide-de-camp (handcuffed to a metallic briefcase). He sits at the table in front and studies his audience.

(NOTE: throughout this and subsequent scenes, a slightly stunned/dazzled quality of uncertainty and disbelief informs the speech, deportment, and expression of the entire cast.)

GENERAL GIBSON
I've just informed the president. He authorized me to read and implement the provisions of National Security Emergency Scrimmage Plan X. Here I go.

The aide-de-camp snaps open the briefcase and passes a nylon pouch to General Gibson. The general opens it and removes a laminated envelope with a plastic seal. He reads a message on the cover:

GENERAL GIBSON
"The following Top Secret directive was mandated into law on July first, 1950."

General Gibson cracks open the seal and withdraws a thin stack of multicolored card-stock pages. He begins:

GENERAL GIBSON
"In the event of unforeseen engagement with intelligent life-form or -forms from any planet not specifically defined as our 'earth', be advised to initiate the following protocols:
(flipping to next card)
(more)

GENERAL GIBSON (cont'd)
One. Confirm said life-form is not operating under the guidance of any hostile foreign terrestrial government."
(pause)
Well, I don't think he's working for the Russians (or the Red Chinese) -- but you never know.

AIDE-DE-CAMP
He certainly didn't give me that impression.

GENERAL GIBSON
(flipping to next card)
"Two. Confirm the life-form does not intend to annex, colonize, vaporize, or expropriate the resources of the sovereign territories of the United States of America."

AIDE-DE-CAMP
I doubt it. He took the asteroid and went.

GENERAL GIBSON
(flipping to next card)
"Three. Identify and detain all possible witnesses and place them under group arrest for a period of no less than one week (defined as seven calendar days), during which time they be subjected to a prescribed battery of medical and psychological examinations and cross-examinations."

AIDE-DE-CAMP
Standard procedure. Already in the works.

GENERAL GIBSON
(flipping to next card)
"Four. Secure the site; cease the dissemination of information; collect and transport the totality of evidence to a hermetically-enclosed/deep-underground secret storage facility; and publicly deny all aspects of the event including its existence for a period of no less than 100 years (defined as 36,500 days)."
End of directive.

GENERAL GIBSON
(unsurprised)
That's pretty clear.

AIDE-DE-CAMP
(also unsurprised)
Ha.

General Gibson passes the stack of cards to the aide-de-camp. He immediately begins running them through a hand-cranked paper shredder. The business executive raises a question:

EXECUTIVE
What do we tell <u>them</u>?

GENERAL GIBSON
Who?

EXECUTIVE
The Junior Stargazers. The Space Cadets. The moms and dads.

AIDE-DE-CAMP
(cheerily)
Midge Campbell.

A murmur among the soldiers. Whispers and tittering. General Gibson thinks. He suggests:

GENERAL GIBSON
Tell them -- it didn't happen?

Silence. Sudden laughter. General Gibson raises an eyebrow, then says gravely:

GENERAL GIBSON
No, obviously, we'll need to formulate a suitable cover story.

INT. LUNCHEONETTE. DAY

The café has been converted into a temporary triage/evaluation unit with dividing screens and curtains on racks and rails. The rivet trailer is parked in front, linked to the front door by a transparent plastic corridor (which ripples in the breeze). Guards outside, scientists inside.

"Station #1: Medical": J.J. and Clifford lie on adjacent gurneys, restrained, wired, and intubated to a bank of beeping/blinking devices registering pulse rate, body temperature, blood oxygen, radiation levels, brainwave patterns, etc. A technician in a lab coat makes a notation on a clipboard and exits. Clifford points to a button on a gadget overtly warning-labeled "DO NOT PRESS" and asks slyly:

CLIFFORD
You dare me? To press that button.

J.J.
No.

CLIFFORD
It's an experiment.

J.J.
(seething)
I'll break your neck.

"Station #2: Psychological": Sandy and Shelly sit side by side at a table facing another technician in a lab coat. The technician displays inkblots and records Shelly's responses in a ledger:

SHELLY
That's an alien doing jumping jacks. That's an alien in a top hat. That's an alien climbing a ladder. That's an alien on a racehorse.

"Station #3: Debriefing": black felt tenting encloses an interrogation booth where Ricky sits in a metal chair under a hot lamp. Two military detectives pace and circle around him. Roger sits silent in the corner, frowning.

DETECTIVE #1
Let's take it from the top.

RICKY
(frustrated)
I told you fifty times. The alien picked up the asteroid --

DETECTIVE #2
(correction)
Alleged alien.

RICKY
(exploding)
I know what I saw!

DETECTIVE #1
It's called a meteorite.

RICKY
An extraterrestrial being.

DETECTIVE #2
(holding up a tiny canister)
This is a microfiche of your school newspaper. Your byline accompanies an article criticizing the principal's disciplinary methods. Who were your sources?

RICKY
(steely)
I was in the sixth grade --

DETECTIVE #2
(angry)
Just answer the question!

RICKY
(enraged)
-- and I will not name names!

The driver/bodyguard, in his corner working on another crossword puzzle, looks up briefly. He takes a bite of a grilled cheese sandwich and resumes his puzzling.

INT. SILO. DAY

A scaffold perch at the top of a metallic staircase. Woodrow stares through a massive telescope out the open bay of the silver dome. He looks up from the eyepiece and squints at the sky, intense and determined. He adjusts focus. On a platform one flight below: Dinah stands next to Dr. Hickenlooper in front of a large model of the meteor crater. She asks:

DINAH
Which way did he go?

Dr. Hickenlooper indicates with a pencil: a low position immediately over the crater; straight up above as high as she can reach; diagonally across the cylindrical room; out the porthole window.

DR. HICKENLOOPER
He went from here. To here. To here.
(quietly/entranced)
To I don't know where.

Woodrow refers to an enormous astronomical map wallpapering all around the interior of the tower as he recalls loudly:

WOODROW
My mother couldn't remember which was which, so she made up her own constellations.
(pointing)
That one's "The Coat Hanger." That one's "The Leaky Faucet." Over there's "Fried Egg with Spatula."

DINAH
(pensive)
My mother is a constellation. At least, part of one. A Swiss scientist named a hypothetical star after her.

DR. HICKENLOOPER
What's it called?

DINAH
Midge Campbell X-9 Major.

Dr. Hickenlooper withdraws a reference book from a shelf and flips pages as she mutters:

DR. HICKENLOOPER
I'll look it up.

WOODROW
(loudly again)
Is she interested in astronomy? Your mother.

DINAH
Not exactly. She's interested in stardom. I don't mean that as a criticism, by the way. It's her job. (To be famous.) Anyway: I'm tired of her face, but I love her voice. She should do more radio.

DR. HICKENLOOPER
(still studying her book)
I never had children. Sometimes I wonder if I wish I should've. (I discovered a hypothetical star myself, by the way.)

DINAH
Which one?

WOODROW
Where is it?

DR. HICKENLOOPER
(pointing)
Right there. It's partly blocked by that burnt-out lightbulb.

Dr. Hickenlooper looks up and down at wallpaper/book in search of Midge Campbell X-9 Major. Dinah ascends the metallic staircase. Woodrow's eyes widen as he sees her clanking up to join him. He chivalrously hops aside to allow her to look through the eyepiece. As Dinah leans into the telescope: Woodrow, transfixed, reverse-bumps into a lever -- then (to catch his balance) slaps his hand onto panel of buttons and knobs -- which sends the entire upper tower into a brisk, humming, shuddering rotation. Woodrow and Dinah straighten, alarmed. The telescope and platform begin to rise/dip and counter-spin. Dr. Hickenlooper shouts up from below:

DR. HICKENLOOPER
Don't spin it around! I had it how I want it. What's happening?

Woodrow and Dinah quickly study the levers, buttons, and knobs. They exchange a look. Together: they click, twist, and pull. The telescope halts with a jolt, banging the two teenagers into each other. They regain their balance and brush themselves off, slightly breathless. An interesting silence; then Woodrow and Dinah simultaneously jolt back toward the telescope, bonk their heads together, then look at each other half-laughing/half-dazed.

WOODROW
After you.

Woodrow motions for Dinah to go first again. He watches (in close-up) as she peers through the telescope: her eyelashes flutter; she licks her lips; she says in a soft voice:

DINAH
Sometimes, I think, mentally: I feel more at home <u>outside</u> the earth's atmosphere.

WOODROW
(enchanted)
Me, too.

INT. MOTEL CABINS #9/10. DAY

Cabin #10: Augie's roller-blind zings open. He is working in his darkroom again, wiggling and fanning another damp print. Cabin #9: Midge, memorizing lines in her own window, watches from across the narrow driveway. Pause.

MIDGE
Did it come out?

AUGIE
(abruptly)
All my pictures come out.

Augie reverses the photograph to show: the alien holding the meteorite (perfectly posed/exposed). Midge squints.

MIDGE
I mean the other one.

Augie hesitates. He looks at the photo. He realizes:

AUGIE
Oh.

Augie hangs the photo of the alien (with clothespins) and produces another new/damp print: the nude of Midge outside her bathroom. It is also excellent. Midge nods, pleased, appreciative. Augie clips it up next to the alien. He sits down in his window. Midge asks abstractly:

MIDGE
You feel different?

AUGIE
(pause)
I don't feel anything at all.

MIDGE
Me, neither.

Silence. Midge says suddenly:

MIDGE
I'm not a good mother.

AUGIE
(hesitates)
Uh-huh.

MIDGE
I love my daughter, but I'm not a good mother, because (unfortunately for her): she's not my first priority. On account of there's always already the thing I plan to do next. I love my daughter, by the way.

AUGIE
Of course. You said.

MIDGE
I love <u>all</u> my children.

MIDGE
We have a magical time when we're together. I have another girl and a boy. They live with my second ex-husband in Utah.

AUGIE
Uh-huh.

MIDGE
He rarely sees them, either.

AUGIE
Uh-huh.

MIDGE
I wish, at least, I felt guilty -- but I don't experience that emotion (if I understand it correctly). I've <u>played</u> it, of course.

AUGIE
(surprised only mildly)
You never feel guilty? In real life.

MIDGE
Not to my knowledge. I think because of my history with violent men (which began with my father, brother, and uncles).

Augie pauses, curious/sympathetic, before choosing not to pursue the matter:

AUGIE
Uh-huh. There's always already the thing I plan to do next, too. Usually, it's a war. Nobody can compete with that. Can they?

MIDGE
(pause)
Probably not. (I did a U.S.O. tour once. It was thrilling.)

Augie tamps and lights his pipe while Midge studies him carefully. Finally, she understands:

MIDGE
I think I see how I see us.

AUGIE
Hm?

MIDGE
I mean, I think I know now what I realize we are: two catastrophically wounded people who don't express the depths of their pain -- because we don't _want_ to. That's our connection. Do you agree?

AUGIE
(long pause)
Uh-huh.

Augie starts to faintly laugh. He mumbles:

AUGIE
Let's change the subject.

Midge laughs faintly, too. A knock on the door of her bedroom.

MIDGE
It's open.

The sound of the door jolting open (off-screen). Stanley's voice calls out:

STANLEY (O.S.)
Hello?

MIDGE
In here.

Pause. Stanley's head peers in through the bathroom door. (He does not see Augie in the window.)

STANLEY
Hello! I'm just your neighbor. Stanley Zak. I wanted to make sure you and your daughter have everything you might need, at the moment.

MIDGE
Thank you. I think so.

STANLEY
What a strange experience this is, isn't it? I went to law school with your former agent, by the way.

MIDGE
Mort?

STANLEY
Mort.

STANLEY
Yes. Mort. Oh --

Stanley has now seen Augie. He frowns slightly and observes the two photographs: alien and nude. About one or the other he says simply:

STANLEY
That came out.

AUGIE
(abruptly again)
All my pictures come out.

The driver/bodyguard appears next to Stanley, suspicious. Stanley frowns. Midge signals: "I'm OK." The driver/bodyguard shrugs. Stanley says coolly:

STANLEY
Anyway, as I say, we're just across the driveway, as my son-in-law seems to have established. Send my best wishes to Mort.

MIDGE
I will.

STANLEY
And his family.

MIDGE
If and when we're permitted contact with the outside world -- though I don't speak to him, to tell you the truth.

STANLEY
I love your hairdo like that.

MIDGE
Thank you.

Stanley lingers.

EXT. MOTEL GARDEN. DAY

The schoolchildren (notebooks and pencil-cases laid out in front of them) occupy one of the picnic tables. June (a bit frazzled) stands next to a blackboard illustrated with a brightly colorful rendering of the solar system in multiple chalk colors. The two chaperones stand by, uneasy. June begins:

JUNE
I'm going to attempt to proceed with the lesson plan I originally prepared. Just to keep orderliness under the circumstances. I expect some of our information about outer space may no longer be completely accurate; but, anyway, there's still only nine planets in the solar system, as far as we know.
(reluctantly)
Billy?

The freckled boy has raised his hand. He blurts:

FRECKLED BOY
Except now there's a' alien!

JUNE
(calmly)
True, by all appearances. Nevertheless: Neptune. Fourth largest planet (by diameter), Neptune orbits the sun only once every 165 years.
(reluctantly)
Bernice?

The little girl with curly red hair has raised her hand. She blurts:

CURLY-HAIRED GIRL
Maybe the alien went there!

JUNE
(calmly)
Well -- maybe? I don't think anybody knows where the alien went or came from.
(reluctantly)
Dwight?

The boy with the cowlick has raised his hand. He says philosophically:

BOY WITH COWLICK
At first, I thought the alien was kind of sneaky, but now I think he was probably nervous to go to earth. He's never been here before, I betch'a.

FRECKLED BOY
(debating)
Then why'd he steal our asteroid then, if he's such a gentleman?

JUNE
(calmly)
These are all reasonable questions; but, at this time, let's stick to Neptune -- because I haven't had time to prepare any lesson plan on this subject we're talking about.

FRECKLED BOY
The alien!

JUNE
The alien, yes. Neptune: named after the god of the sea, of course -- and, by the way, I'm not trying to evade your questions. I want to emphasize: you're safe. We all are. (Here on earth.) Your parents have been notified of, at least, something. America remains at peace.
(surprised)
Yes, Montana?

Montana appears next to June. He takes off his cowboy hat and holds it like a suitor as he proposes:

MONTANA
I'd like to parley a notion, myself, if I could, June.

June hesitates. She nods. Montana addresses the class in a gentle, thoughtful, protective voice:

MONTANA
I figger this here alien come from a tribe we don't know nothin' 'bout, do we? Anything we say'd just be pure speckalation! But I tell you what I reckon: I reckon that alien don't mean no harm 'tall. I reckon he just took hisself down here to have a looksy at the land
(more)

MONTANA (cont'd)
and the peoples on it. In the spirit a' exploration. See, I don't look on a feller alien all suspicious-like. No, he ain't American; no, he ain't a creature a God's green earth; but he's a creature a somewheres -- and so're we. Now let's show the ol' feller some hospitality, and if he turns out to be a dirty dog (which I reckon he ain't), well, that'll be a job for the United States armed forces, and they ain't never lost a war yet. Thanky-do.

Montana puts his hat back on and smiles to June and the schoolchildren. June looks at Montana with both puzzlement and admiration. She touches his dusty arm briefly. She says to the group:

JUNE
I agree with Montana. Now: Neptune.

EXT. DESERT. DAY

Outside the fence at the rear the motel: the motel manager explains the terms of a sale to J.J. as Clifford stands beside them doing tricks with his yo-yo. J.J. clutches a paper from the vending machine: "Deed of Sale."

MOTEL MANAGER
You see that wonderful crackly-patch right out there between the dead cactuses and the dried-up riverbed?

J.J.
I think so.

MOTEL MANAGER
That's your parcel.

The motel manager sweeps his arm slowly toward the barren nothingness, marveling. J.J. squints.

J.J.
How much of it? Do I own.

MOTEL MANAGER
Well, it's actually an interesting financial mechanism. You don't technically own anything outright. You own stock in the town. In the form of a loan. With a fifty year maturity rate. Then: at the end -- the loan is forgiven.

Clifford pockets his yo-yo. He chimes in:

CLIFFORD
You dare me?

J.J. ignores the question. He continues the real-estate discussion:

J.J.
How about water?

MOTEL MANAGER
(hesitates)
Of course, I understand. There isn't any. This is a desert opportunity.

J.J. looks skeptical. Clifford attempts to reiterate:

CLIFFORD
You dare me?

J.J.
I heard you.

CLIFFORD
It's an experiment.

J.J.
(interrupting)
I don't care anymore. I dare you, or I don't dare you. It doesn't matter. Do what you wish. I give up.

Clifford goes silent, wounded. The motel manager, curious, looks back and forth between father and son. J.J. asks Clifford sincerely:

J.J.
What's the cause? What's the meaning? Why do you always have to <u>dare</u> something?

CLIFFORD
(long pause)
I don't know. Maybe it's because I'm afraid, otherwise, nobody'll -- notice -- my existence -- in the universe?

Silence. J.J. turns to the motel manager. The motel manager nods slowly. They both turn to Clifford. Clifford shrugs and sniffles. He looks like he is about to cry (but does not). Suddenly:

J.J.
Dare you what?

MOTEL MANAGER
Dare you what?

CLIFFORD
(sadly)
To climb that cactus out there.

J.J.
(adamant)
Lord, no.

MOTEL MANAGER
(worried)
Please, don't.

Clifford, perhaps out of a sense of obligation, walks deliberately toward a high cactus in the middle-distance.

EXT. HIGHWAY. DAY

Augie and Stanley flank Woodrow (in a mystified reverie) as they walk down the center of the roadblocked highway through the little town. The three girls trail behind them, stalking a dragonfly with a butterfly net. Further in the background: troops drill patrol along the barricades.

AUGIE
If I sleep on a cot instead of the sofa-bed that might leave room for me to set up a darkroom in the pool house. Is that possible? As a compromise.

STANLEY
Depends on the measurements. I can actually carpool the girls to school by golf-cart, you know. If I cut across the fourteenth tee.

AUGIE
(surprised)
It's that close? The elementary.

WOODROW
(in disbelief)
How can you two even <u>think</u> about this? The world will never be the same!

Augie and Stanley nod, sympathetic rather than deeply engaged. Woodrow continues:

WOODROW
What happens next? Nobody knows! Will he visit us again? Will he speak to us? What will he say? Why did he steal our asteroid? Was it ours in the first place? Does he -- <u>like</u> us? Nobody knows!

AUGIE
That's true.

WOODROW
(re: the universe)
What's out there? <u>Some</u>thing! The meaning of life? Maybe there <u>is</u> one!

Stanley frowns. He says to Woodrow:

STANLEY
I hope you're still Episcopalian.

Woodrow ignores this question. He says, electrified:

WOODROW
You took his picture, Dad!

Augie nods. He shrugs. Woodrow drifts away, looking up at the sky and writing in his notebook. Augie sits on the hood of his now-derelict station wagon. He says to Stanley genuinely:

AUGIE
You really want us, Stanley?

STANLEY
(bluntly)
No, but you need me.

AUGIE
(long pause)
She did love me, you know.

STANLEY
Who says she didn't? I've been on my own for twelve years, after all (and, remember: my wife drank herself to death).

AUGIE
(pause)
I don't know what that means.

Stanley sits next to Augie. He says carefully:

STANLEY
In my loneliness (or, perhaps, because of it), I've learned not to judge people; to take people as I find them, not as others find them; and, most of all, to give complete and unquestioning faith to the people I love. That doesn't include you, but it included my daughter -- and your four children -- and you're welcome to stay with me as long as you wish, whether I like it or not (which I don't, by the way).

Augie grits his teeth. Stanley takes a deep breath. Augie stage-whispers:

AUGIE
Stop helping us. We're in grief!

Stanley, puzzled, stage-whispers back:

STANLEY
Me, too!

Stanley grips Augie by the shoulders and shakes him gently in mock/genuine frustration. Woodrow suddenly re-appears. He points a finger at his father.

WOODROW
Are you planning to abandon us?

Long pause. Stanley looks baffled. Augie says eventually:

AUGIE
I <u>was</u> (as a temporary measure) --

STANLEY
(stunned)
What?

AUGIE
-- but I decided against it.

WOODROW
I knew it. I sensed it.

STANLEY
<u>I</u> didn't!

Augie and Stanley debate briefly, aside:

AUGIE
I would've hired a babysitter. In addition to you.

STANLEY
I'm the grandfather. I'm not the wet nurse.

Augie returns his attention to Woodrow. He clarifies:

AUGIE
I'm not planning to abandon you. Anymore. Even as a temporary measure (which is all it ever would've been).

WOODROW
I forgive you for considering it.

Woodrow drifts away again. Augie takes a deep breath. He looks at the girls and asks:

AUGIE
What about you?

ANDROMEDA
We're going to sleep under the floor of the house in a secret prison powered by electricity from an erupting volcano.

AUGIE
OK. Who needs to pee? Let's go inside and order some chili.

EXT. METEOR CRATER. EVENING

The crater floor remains decorated exactly as last seen during the alien's brief visit (including picnic blankets, root beer, peanuts, viewing devices); but hundreds of tags and markers stuck in the dirt now indicate names, times, distances, and other statistical information. An empty divot where the meteorite previously sat is now taped off and isolated -- as is the pair of peculiar footprints next to it. Guards stand at attention while men in rubber suits search with metal detectors, scan with Geiger counters, take rock and soil samples, analyze atmospheric conditions, etc. Cameras and recording devices flutter and hum. General Gibson, at his lectern, explains to a small team of assembled scientists and military personnel (including Dr. Hickenlooper) over the P.A. speaker:

GENERAL GIBSON
For the official Military-science Division archive: this is a forensic re-enactment of events that occurred on this site exactly sixteen hours ago --
(checking his watch)
-- now.

General Gibson puts on his viewing device. Everyone else follows suit.

GENERAL GIBSON
Dr. Hickenlooper, would you like to repeat the remarks you said yesterday? To the best of your recollection.

DR. HICKENLOOPER
Well, I began by describing various properties of the Astronomical Ellipses.
(suddenly)
What's that noise?

The general silence has been broken by the sound of prominent, crunchy chewing. Dr. Hickenlooper lifts the corner of her viewing device and peers out. From inside the box on his head, the aide-de-camp says with his mouth full of food:

AIDE-DE-CAMP
Fritos.

DR. HICKENLOOPER
(frowning)
Were you eating those last night? When the alien came.

AIDE-DE-CAMP
How could I? The snack machine was turned off.

DR. HICKENLOOPER
Then give it.

The aide-de-camp reluctantly hands his package of corn chips to Dr. Hickenlooper. Dr. Hickenlooper clears her throat and presses on:

DR. HICKENLOOPER
Twice every fifty-seven years, when the earth, the sun, the moon, and the galactic plane of the Milky Way --

AIDE-DE-CAMP
(suddenly)
What's that contraption?

The aide-de-camp points to: the mechanic, nearby, cradling the cast-iron assembly which fell from the underside of Augie's car. He explains to Dr. Hickenlooper and General Gibson:

MECHANIC
I've never seen an assembly of this kind on any American make or model (nor foreign, actually) in all my experience. I thought maybe it might be some kind of hot rod power-booster (unusual for a station wagon); but, then, after what occurred and so on, I figured it's my duty to bring it to the attention of the proper authorities. In case it comes from outer space.

General Gibson examines the assembly. He muses:

GENERAL GIBSON
It might be from space, or it might be from earth. Impossible to tell.
(to the executive)
What do you think?

EXECUTIVE
No idea.

GENERAL GIBSON
(to the aide-de-camp)
Put it in a box and mark it: "unknown."

AIDE-DE-CAMP
Yes, sir. Like we always do.

Dr. Hickenlooper looks at General Gibson and the executive, skeptical. She continues her address (now eating corn chips as she speaks):

DR. HICKENLOOPER
After that, I said something like, "Boy, aren't these just luminously marvelous colors?" Then I warned everybody not to look right at it.

EXT. HIGHWAY. NIGHT

After dark. The middle of the town, quiet and empty. A guard sits in a chair in front of the telephone booth. A sign on a barricade behind him reads:

Public Telephone Service Suspended
Official Use Only
by order of
the United States Military-science
Research and Experimentation Division

The night wind blows gently. Moths flutter under a roadside lamp. Clifford saunters out of the dimness, practicing his yo-yo. (His face and hands are now covered with numerous, tiny bandages.) He approaches the guard and smiles.

CLIFFORD
Evening, Chief.

The guard nods, blank. Clifford finishes an offhand trick then pockets his yo-yo.

CLIFFORD
Can I ask you to stick this dime in the payphone for me, please?

Clifford holds out a dime. The guard answers, stony:

GUARD
All public telephone service has been suspended until further notice.

CLIFFORD
I know it. The thing is: right before the hubbub yesterday, I made a trunk call to my cousin (long distance), and the
(more)

CLIFFORD (cont'd)
operator let me owe the surcharge because all I had was three pennies. I don't feel right stealing from the telephone company.

Silence. The guard shrugs. He takes the dime, unlocks/opens a special triple-latch on the door of the telephone booth, and reaches inside to slip the dime into its slot. The dime clinks. The payphone clacks. The guard closes the door and re-locks it.

Camera booms up: through the roof of the little booth, diagonally along the telephone line up to the top of a nearby utility pole, horizontally across the parking area and motor court gardens -- to a jerry-rigged junction spliced with clamps, clips, and electrical tape which branches off and descends down (via what appears to be a pair of automobile jumper cables) into Tent #7.

The exterior wall of the tent dissolves away to reveal, inside: a tidy, canvas motel room on a wooden platform floor with braided rugs. It is furnished exactly as the surrounding cabins. Ricky, wearing a radio headset, listens at a complicated, improvised telecommunications console. Woodrow, Dinah, and Shelly sit beside him, waiting. Woodrow and Dinah are in mid-conversation, animated:

DINAH
Although it might convey a different meaning on _his_ planet.

WOODROW
That's true -- if he even _has_ a planet, by the way! He might be nomadic?

Dinah considers this. Ricky's eyes light up. He holds up his finger for silence.

RICKY
Operator? Kismet-nine, seven-seven-oh. Station to station. Thank you.

Clifford pokes his head through the tent flap. Ricky looks at him and nods. Clifford slips inside.

SPLIT-SCREEN:

On one side: Ricky with the others in the tent. On the other side: a telephone rings in a suburban kitchen. A carefully coiffed and made-up mother, svelte in a stylish dress and apron, dries her hands on a dishtowel as she picks up the receiver and answers, a bit sharp:

MOTHER
Hello? Who's calling?

RICKY
Good evening, Mrs. Weatherford. It's Ricky Cho. May I have a word with --

MOTHER
(checking her watch)
It's after nine, Ricky. He's already drinking his Ovaltine. Can't this wait until tomorrow?

RICKY
(unfortunately)
I'm afraid not, Mrs. Weatherford. I wouldn't disturb you if it weren't of the utmost importance to the *Weekly Bobcat*. I just need a minute of his time.

MOTHER
(pause)
All right, Ricky. Hold the line.

The mother exits. Ricky looks to his colleagues; Clifford distributes Raisinets; Shelly asks Woodrow and Dinah (a bit blunt):

SHELLY
Some kind of romance between the two of you?

Woodrow turns bright red again. He says:

WOODROW
Who?

SHELLY
Who. You.

DINAH
(coolly)
Who?

SHELLY
(louder)
You know who!

WOODROW
(flustered)
Us?

DINAH
(evenly)
We only met yesterday.

WOODROW
(mortified)
I feel she doesn't like me in that way.

Dinah looks at Woodrow briefly, calm. Woodrow takes a deep breath. Shelly concludes:

SHELLY
Uh-huh. Well, I think you're pretty smart, but I think you're pretty dumb.

In the meantime: a sleepy boy in pajamas and a tartan bathrobe enters the kitchen (sipping a glass of warm/chocolatey milk with a straw) and picks up the receiver:

SLEEPY BOY
Hello?

RICKY
(to the others:)
Shh!
(to the sleepy boy:)
Skip? Ricky. We got a scoop.

INT. TELEVISION STUDIO. DAY

Black and white.

The lights come up on another set: a rehearsal space in a converted cast-iron building (formerly a garment factory). Sprung wooden floor, low platform stage, pressed tin ceiling. One wall of expansive windows looks out at a painted theatrical background depicting an elevated train station platform; another wall is fully mirrored like a dance studio. Wooden chairs seat twenty students, aged twenty-five to forty, well-dressed in jackets with neckties and skirts with scarves. Some smoke cigarettes. One of them is the host. He turns briefly to address camera:

HOST
The first hints of the future existence of "Asteroid City" were revealed during a special seminar scheduled at the playwright's request.

The teacher/guru, shoeless in a narrow suit of Communist origin, bright-eyed and commanding, sits perched on a threadbare but comfortable settee. He begins (in faintly mittel-Europa accent):

TEACHER
Conrad Earp: how can we help you?

The playwright, seated on the stage alone, answers, hopeful:

PLAYWRIGHT
Well, the thing is, Saltzie: I'd like to make a scene where all my characters are each gently/privately seduced into the
(more)

PLAYWRIGHT (cont'd)
deepest, dreamiest slumber of their lives as a result of their shared experience of a bewildering and bedazzling celestial mystery --

TEACHER
(interrupting)
A sleeping scene.

PLAYWRIGHT
(reluctantly clarifying)
A scene of sleeping -- but I don't know how to write it!

TEACHER
Yet.

PLAYWRIGHT
Yet. I thought, perhaps, if you and your wonderfully talented pupils just improvise? Something might reveal itself.

The host stands up and moves among the students as he continues his narration:

HOST
Who wasn't going to be famous? On any given day: roll-call in Saltzburg Keitel's classroom was a now-dazzling list of undiscovered luminaries:

The host points out various notable figures: the actor who plays Roger, the actress who plays Shelly, the actor who plays the mechanic, the actor who plays Montana, the actress who plays Midge -- and (behind them all, in the corner of the back row, seated on the floor, near the door) the actor who plays Augie.

HOST
Linus Mao, Lucretia Shaver, Walter Geronimo, Asquith Eden, Mercedes Ford. Even, unofficially: Jones Hall.

The actor who plays Roger raises his hand to ask:

ACTOR/ROGER
What's it about? The play.

PLAYWRIGHT
(pause)
Infinity, and I don't know what else.

The actress who plays Shelly chimes in:

ACTRESS/SHELLY
Is there a title?

PLAYWRIGHT
I'm torn. Perhaps: "The Cosmic Wilderness." Do you like that one?

ACTRESS/MIDGE
Not really.

The room echoes in agreement. The actor who plays Montana asks (in an English accent):

ACTOR/MONTANA
What's the other? Title, I mean.

PLAYWRIGHT
It's the name of the small town on the California/Nevada/Arizona desert where the story takes place.

The teacher rises from his settee and begins to prowl the stage, ruminating. He demands:

TEACHER
Who here has fallen asleep ever onstage during a live performance? In front of a paying audience.

A voice answers from an unseen corner of the room:

DIRECTOR (O.S.)
Me.

The teacher and his students all turn to see: the director. The director smiles slyly. So does the teacher. Students whisper.

DIRECTOR
I spent the first three-quarters of Act II of "The Welterweight" on a massage table with no lines until the last minute and a half. One night, I nodded off.

TEACHER
On purpose? You did this.

DIRECTOR
(absolutely not)
No.

TEACHER
Did you miss your cue?

DIRECTOR
Almost. I heard it, and I woke up (very scared) -- but I knew my lines.

Silence. The teacher tips an imaginary hat.

TEACHER
Good morning, Schubert.

DIRECTOR
Good morning, Saltzie.

TEACHER
What brings you here today? Haven't seen you in six weeks.

DIRECTOR
"Lavender and Lemons" opened last night (to very good, I might say, raves, by the way). I'm available.

Both the teacher and the director now look significantly to the playwright: available. The director says quietly:

DIRECTOR
Hello, Connie.

The playwright nods, demure and pleased. The host, now behind/beside the teacher, director, and playwright, interjects:

HOST
What did he teach? Example:

TEACHER
Sleep: is not death. The body keeps busy (breathing air, pumping blood, thinking). Maybe you pay visit to your dead mother. Maybe you go to bed with ex-wife. Or husband! Maybe you climb the Matterhorn. Connie: you wake up with new scene three-quarters written in the head already. Schubert: you wake up with a hangover. Important things happen. Is there something to play? I think so. Let's work on scene from the outside in: be inert -- then dream.

On cue: the students all go inert -- then dream: yawning, snoring, sleepwalking/sleeptalking, tossing and turning, singing a lullaby, thumbsucking with a security blanket, etc. The teacher turns to the playwright and says, shouting over the din:

TEACHER
Where are we, Connie? And <u>when</u>. Talk to us!

PLAYWRIGHT
(startled)
All right.

As the playwright speaks, the lights begin to slowly fade -- leaving him alone, spotlit in the darkness:

PLAYWRIGHT
One week later. Our cast of characters' already tenuous grasp of reality has further slipped in quarantine, and the group begins to occupy a space of the most peculiar emotional dimensions. Meanwhile: the information blockade spearheaded by General Grif Gibson has been, it appears, incomplete...

EXT. HIGHWAY. DAY

Widescreen/color.

In all directions encircling the town: an ambush of press and public (beyond/outside the military barricades). Television crews; radio reporters; newspapermen and women; visitors by the dozen with picnic baskets and transistor radios; vendors selling popcorn, toy meteorites, and postcards of a crude but generally accurate rendering of the alien with the meteorite tucked under his arm (evidently based on Ricky's description). Parked cars, trucks, and vans everywhere. Campers camping. A Ferris wheel. An arriving passenger train bannered "Asteroid City Alien Special" jammed with tourists leaning out windows and clambering down from doors -- among them a newsboy carrying a stack of papers. He shouts:

NEWSBOY
Extra! Extra! Late Edition!

INSERT:

The front page of a daily newspaper (*The Arid Plains Desert Post*). Headline: "High School Student Breaks Alien Invasion Story: Exposes Military Cover-up." A sidebar begins: "Junior Stargazer, Ace Reporter: Ricky Cho (of the Coldcreek High School *Weekly Bobcat*)." Augie's photograph of the alien is top/center with a caption: Augie Steenbeck/French Press International.

INT. OBSERVATORY. DAY

The classroom. General Gibson sits, as before, at the table in front. Ricky, in a school desk, faces him. Also present: Roger, the business executive, two guards. (Tacked to the wall: numerous photographs of the alien's footprints.) General Gibson is offended, disappointed, angry:

GENERAL GIBSON
I hope you're aware: you and your accomplices may still face felony prosecution. Possibly, even, a treason charge.

RICKY
(unfazed)
I'll fight it all the way to the Supreme Court, if necessary -- and win.

The door opens, and the aide-de-camp enters to deliver a yellow envelope to General Gibson.

AIDE-DE-CAMP
This just in: from the president.

General Gibson tears open the envelope. He speed-reads a telegram. He tosses papers fluttering into the air as he groans, wounded:

GENERAL GIBSON
He's furious. Thanks, Ricky.

ROGER
(sympathetic)
I don't know what to say, General Gibson. I'm sorry.

RICKY
Don't apologize, Dad. The public has a right to the truth.

ROGER
(gently)
You made your point.

RICKY
(shouting)
This tribunal is a mockery!

Ricky strides to the door, father in tow. The business executive inquires, aside, to General Gibson:

EXECUTIVE
What about Steenbeck? Who took the photograph. It's on the front page of every newspaper on the planet. Can't we arrest him, as well?

GENERAL GIBSON
Unfortunately, no. He dropped a print in the mail (to his photo-agency) first thing Tuesday morning, and the postman got it before we did. He's innocent. Supposedly, he did a nude of Midge Campbell, too.

EXT. DESERT. DAY

An improvised shooting range behind the luncheonette. A barrage of machine-gun bullets rips into a row of paper targets (adapted from Augie's alien photograph) pinned to a bank of hay bales, shredding them. A dozen soldiers, flat on the ground in a row, quickly reload. One of them (the guard from the telephone booth) notices something off-screen and frowns.

A hundred yards away: a beer bottle catapults into the air. J.J. hoists Clifford's electromagnetic death-ray up to his shoulder and pulls the trigger, silently zapping the bottle into glowing dots which linger/sizzle/pop. J.J. recharges the death-ray while Sandy observes at his side. Stanley distributes fresh martinis from the cantina machine. (He retains another round in his free hand, clasped by a finger in each cup.)

SANDY
How long can they keep us in Asteroid City? Legally, I mean.

J.J.
Well, I'm not an attorney, but I'd say: "As long as they like." I think we'd have to file an injunction and successfully argue the case. Six months to a year? Of course, we'd also initiate a civil suit for loss of income.

STANLEY
(pleasantly)
Maybe we should just walk out right now. I'm not sure they can stop us. Without killing somebody.

J.J.
Interesting idea. What kind of mileage you think that jet pack gets?

SANDY
(taking the death-ray)
Ask Roger (or his son). Apparently, he's being prosecuted for revealing state secrets.

J.J.
(dismissive)
They'll never make it stick.

STANLEY
I'm in no hurry. I like the desert. I like aliens.

J.J. places another beer bottle into the launcher and catapults it. Sandy aims the death-ray -- but an off-screen voice interrupts brusquely:

GUARD (O.S.)
How'd you get that back?

J.J., Sandy, and Stanley turn suddenly, startled. (The bottle falls to the ground, unzapped, and shatters.) The telephone booth guard (still armed for target practice) stands behind the group. J.J. retrieves the death-ray from Sandy, possessive.

GUARD
The projects remain under secure lockdown. No Stargazer is permitted personal access without the express permission --

J.J.
(righteous)
My son invented this death-ray.

GUARD
(hesitates)
That may be true; but my orders --

The guard reaches toward the death-ray. J.J. swings up the nose of the device.

J.J.
Step back!

STANLEY
(concerned/bemused)
Easy, fellas. We're not in Guadalcanal anymore.

The aide-de-camp jogs briskly from another direction to intervene. He carries a military-issue handheld two-way radio. He says soothingly:

AIDE-DE-CAMP
OK! Calm down, please. Everybody. It's been a difficult quarantine.

J.J. and the guard are now pointing their weapons at each other, point-blank. They shout/scream:

GUARD
You stole your projects!

J.J.
I'll zap you right now!

The aide-de-camp's radio crackles: "Stand down!" The aide-de-camp nods and says sharply to the guard:

AIDE-DE-CAMP
Stand down! You see? General Gibson says, "Stand down." We'll re-confiscate the projects at a later time. Probably after dinner.

J.J.
(grimly)
Try it.

INT. MOTEL CABINS #9/10. DAY

Cabin #10: Augie's roller-blind zings open once again as he wiggles/fans another damp print. (Hanging from clothespins behind him: a print of the Steenbeck family station wagon on blocks.) He says loudly without looking:

AUGIE
This was on an old roll I forgot to develop in the glove box.

Augie reverses the photograph to show: himself in a smoky/misty jungle, hair matted with blood, more blood caked black on the side of his neck, puffing his pipe, holding up a bloody/twisty metal shard.

AUGIE
"Self-portrait with Shrapnel."

As he hangs the print Augie finally sees in Cabin #9, across the driveway: Midge, lifeless in an overflowing bathtub with an empty bottle of sleeping pills spilled all over the floor. Augie freezes, squints, and stares. Midge says motionless, eyes closed, mascara streaked:

MIDGE
Do page forty-five.

Augie hesitates. He disappears briefly -- then returns holding a copy of Midge's script. He sits and reads out loud:

AUGIE
"What've you done? How could you?"

MIDGE
It says, "shouting and crying."

AUGIE
Uh-huh.

MIDGE
So shout and cry.

AUGIE
(shouting/crying)
"How could you!

MIDGE
(evenly)
How couldn't I?

AUGIE
(stupefied)
How -- couldn't -- you?

MIDGE
That's what I'm asking.

AUGIE
(wounded)
It was over. Already. You were free. What's the point of committing suicide when there's nothing left to escape?

MIDGE
(opening her eyes)
Maybe that was the problem all along."

AUGIE
(out of character)
Now it says I smash everything off the shelf.

MIDGE
So smash everything off the --

Augie makes shattering/crashing sounds and bashes imaginary plates and vases off imaginary shelves in every direction, enraged. He reels back to Midge and says, baffled:

AUGIE
"Such a sickening waste. Think of the people. Think of the places. Think of the --"

MIDGE
(directing)
Use your grief.

AUGIE
(stiffening)
For a rehearsal? I'm not even in this picture. I'm a war photographer.

Midge shrugs. Long pause. Augie tries again, crushed/heartbroken -- and improved:

AUGIE
"Such a sickening waste. Think of the people. Think of the places. Think of the world you could've seen, Dolores.

MIDGE
(inevitably)
I've already seen it."

AUGIE
(out of character)
Is she a ghost?

MIDGE
It's not clear.

AUGIE
(skimming/paraphrasing)
Then the coroner comes in. Orders me out of the room. I slowly turn away and close the door. Scene. My sandwich is burning.

Augie stands up and exits the bathroom. Camera dollies to the next window to reveal Augie forking a grilled cheese from a hot plate on the table. Midge enters her own bedroom (opposing window), wrapping her dressing gown around her as she sits. She says, suddenly tense:

MIDGE
My daughter saw us.

AUGIE
(alarmed)
What?

MIDGE
Dinah saw us. Through this window. In your bedroom yesterday.

AUGIE
(resourceful)
Did you tell her we were rehearsing again?

MIDGE
(regretful)
I didn't think of that. I should've. Now it's too late, because I admitted everything.

AUGIE
(short pause, uneasy)
Did she tell Woodrow?

MIDGE
Hard to say. She can keep a secret. I don't know if she will.

Augie and Midge simultaneously look away and sigh. Midge begins to carefully funnel sleeping pills back into their bottle. She says quietly:

MIDGE
This isn't the beginning of something, Augie.

AUGIE
(pause)
Isn't it?

MIDGE
(surprised)
Is it?

AUGIE
(resigned)
Probably not.

Another pause. Then, simultaneously:

AUGIE
(hopeful/desperate)
Although you never know.

MIDGE
(hopeful/affectionate)
Unless maybe it is?

Augie and Midge stare at each other. Augie says oddly:

AUGIE
I don't like the way that guy looked at us.

MIDGE
(not following)
Which guy?

AUGIE
The alien.

MIDGE
(surprised)
Oh. How'd he --

AUGIE
(interrupting)
Like we're doomed.

A beat. Augie looks down to:

INSERT:

The electric hot plate (patterned with diagonal zig-zag lightning bolts). Brand: "Quicky-Griddle."

Augie slaps down his palm on the burner. He yelps and jerks his hand away. Midge frowns.

MIDGE
What'd you just do?

AUGIE
(frozen)
I burned my hand on the Quicky-Griddle.

MIDGE
(confused)
Why?

AUGIE
It's not clear.

MIDGE
(deeply perplexed)
Show me.

Augie holds up his hand. The palm is seared with griddled lightning bolts. Midge looks shocked.

MIDGE
You really did it! That actually happened.

Augie looks at his hand, bewildered. He frowns.

EXT. MOTEL GARDEN. DAY

The schoolchildren sit, once again, at their picnic table. June (now wearing slightly more make-up than usual, with one extra blouse button unbuttoned and her hair looser, in waves) stands next to her blackboard which is still illustrated with the colorful solar system and now includes numerous moons and detailed size/distance/mass measurements. The two chaperones remain uneasy.

The motel gardener/handyman studies a user's manual and tinkers with pliers and screwdrivers behind a large cabinet housing a tiny television screen (tuned to static) situated on a rolling cart. Adjacent: a pedestal-mounted television camera. June begins:

JUNE
As you know, boys and girls, your parents arrived late last night by military helicopter. They've been sequestered in that metal hut over there --

June points to, just outside the town perimeter/barricades, between throngs of festive visitors: a mobile Quonset hut with a Sikorsky helicopter parked next to it.

JUNE
-- for the past several hours while the government scientists explain the situation to them (although everything's already in the newspapers). It's my understanding they're about to go onto this closed-circuit television set? At any moment.

GARDENER/HANDYMAN
Everything's connected, but nothing's working.

The gardener/handyman continues to tinker. June continues:

JUNE
Let's carry on with the lesson plan, then. Jupiter:
(reluctantly)
Billy?

The freckled boy has raised his hand. He blurts:

FRECKLED BOY
I did the alien's flying saucer with a hubcap and a chicken pot pie tin.

The freckled boy displays an intricately constructed scale model of the alien's spacecraft (employing toothpicks, paperclips, sequins, glitter, pipe cleaners, and cotton ball smoke). A critical/appreciative murmur among the other schoolchildren.

JUNE
Good work. Very accurate. Fifth planet from the sun, largest in our solar system, Jupiter --
(reluctantly)
Bernice?

The girl with curly red hair has raised her hand. She blurts:

CURLY-HAIRED GIRL
I did the alien on his home planet.

The curly-haired girl displays a crayon drawing of the alien (in thinker-pose, mysteriously smiling) perched on a rock in front of a futuristic mansion in a barren desert. Another critical/appreciative murmur.

JUNE
Well done. How wonderful. Due to extreme atmospheric conditions, an anticyclonic storm has raged on Jupiter's surface for over --
(reluctantly)
Dwight?

The boy with the cowlick has raised his hand. He blurts:

BOY WITH COWLICK
I wrote a song about him.

The boy with the cowlick displays a wide-ruled sheet of pencilled lyrics. June hesitates, uneasy.

JUNE
Oh. Um. This may not be the time for a musical performance. Let's --
(surprised)
Yes, Montana?

Montana appears next to June (again), tuning a rattly lap-steel guitar as the entire posse of other cowboys and ranch hands filters into formation behind him, briskly arranging several hay bales and tuning their own instruments. The boy with the cowlick steps in front. Montana explains:

MONTANA
Pardon th' interuption, June. The boys and I heard ol' Dwight was scribblin' up a little warble, so we learned ourselves to play it.

The group launches directly into a haunting western chant with ominous, plucked accompaniment. The boy with the cowlick steeples his hands as if in prayer and sings:

BOY WITH COWLICK
Dear alien, who art in heaven,
Lean and skinny, 'bout six-foot-seven;
Though we know ye ain't our brother:
Are you friend or foe (or other)?

The chorus brings the song instantly into the upbeat skiffle/rodeo genre with full country orchestration and the entire posse singing in unison (in three octaves):

CHORUS
Hop on one foot,
Skip on two;
Dance the Spaceman,
Howdly-do!
Bounce on four foot,
Spring on three;
Let's be Spacemen,
(in twelve-part harmony:)
Howdly-dee!

The children, ecstatic, clap and bounce with the joyful music. Montana sets aside his lap-steel, hops over to June, takes her hand, and pulls her into a dance while the other musicians (and, now, the gardener/handyman, as well) continue to play a round of exquisite/repeated "Howdly-dees!" with whoops and stomps etc. June, caught off-guard, laughs as Montana swings her in a circle. Unobserved on the T.V. set: the parents (clustered together inside a small hangar, hot, haggard, weary, unkempt, slightly terrified) have finally been connected. They watch, mystified.

(NOTE: the lyric "or other" might, perhaps, be sung by one of the ranch hands in extreme, deepest *basso profondo*.)

EXT. MOTEL CABIN #7. DAY

The five teenagers sit together (once again) in a circle on the ground between the burned ruins and the canvas tent. One of the radio telescopes from the field outside the observatory has been relocated into the immediate background. It spins quietly in its familiar manner. As Dinah lists names (periodically pointing to Ricky, Clifford, and/or Shelly as "out"), Dr. Hickenlooper appears (unnoticed) behind them. She inspects the radio telescope, surprised/irritated. She watches the game briefly.

(NOTE: Woodrow and Dinah, the only players not "out," stare only at each other during the game. The other participants look back and forth between them, invested in the outcome of the competition -- but also intrigued by the noticeable chemistry in the air. Clifford performs an occasional yo-yo trick.)

DINAH
-- Tab Hunter, Doris Day, out, Jack the Ripper, out, Bing Crosby, Shirley Temple, out, out, Orson Welles, Lucille Ball, out, Marlon Brando, out, Queen Elizabeth, Mickey Mantle, out, out, Yul Bryner, Louis Armstrong, out, Lana Turner, out --

Dr. Hickenlooper follows a low, suspended electrical cable into the tent. Camera dollies with her to reveal: a much-expanded array of sophisticated gadgetry and wiring (humming, blinking, beeping) which now fills the entire space beyond its capacity. (Dinah's plant-growing device appears to have cultivated a beanstalk which extends out through a hole in the roof of the tent.) Dr. Hickenlooper shakes her head. She returns to the group while Dinah continues:

DINAH
-- Betty Grable, Ella Fitzgerald, out, out, Rock Hudson, out, Jerry Lewis, out, out --

DR. HICKENLOOPER
(interrupting)
Who's responsible for stealing my radio telescope, my signal-processing receiver, and my entire spectrographical monitoring network?

The five startled teenagers look to each other, worried. Woodrow answers:

WOODROW
We're trying to contact the alien.

Dr. Hickenlooper struggles to convey the depths of her profoundly wounded annoyance as she responds:

DR. HICKENLOOPER
I appreciate that -- but what about Dr. Hickenlooper? I personally designed most of this equipment. I lobbied for congressional support. I cultivated dubious relationships in the private sector (a necessary compromise). Plus: I sit up there in my observatory every night. Watching and listening. If you're trying to contact the alien: include <u>me</u>!
(pause)
Did you hear anything from him? So far.

WOODROW
No.

Dr. Hickenlooper scoffs: "Ha." She motions with a thumb back towards the tent:

DR. HICKENLOOPER
The squiggle control is disabled, by the way.

RICKY
(speculating)
We thought that might reduce resistance in the secondary circuit.

DR. HICKENLOOPER
(pause)
I doubt it. If you want to borrow my stuff, ask first. What's all this?

Dr. Hickenlooper points. Camera pans slightly to reveal a bulletin board displaying a large concept-drawing which depicts the moon with the American flag projected onto it; and, thumb-tacked around it, alternative symbols: a cross, a Star of David, a pentagram, an eye, a pyramid, a yin/yang, the Coca-Cola logo, and the photograph of Woodrow's mother. Woodrow explains:

WOODROW
I put the American flag just to be patriotic. Now we need to really <u>mean</u> something. A universal message. Not only to earthlings.

RICKY
We already thought of everything we could think of: a cross, a star, a four-leaf-clover; letters, numbers, hieroglyphics.

DR. HICKENLOOPER
(pause)
What's the point of projecting a star onto the moon?

WOODROW
Exactly.

DR. HICKENLOOPER
I ask that sincerely.

SHELLY
(hopeful)
How about "$E=mc^2$?" I still think --

DINAH	CLIFFORD
They know that.	It's too easy.

WOODROW
This is our chance to be actually -- worthwhile. In our lifetimes.

DR. HICKENLOOPER
(long pause)
I see what you mean. Whose turn was it?

DINAH
The middle of mine. I better start over. Cleopatra, Jagadish Chandra Bose, Antonie van Leeuwenhoek, Paracelsus, Kurt Gödel, William Henry Bragg, Lord Kelvin, Midge Campbell, Konstantin Tsiolkovsky --

As Dinah effortlessly continues down her list, Dr. Hickenlooper signals for Woodrow to join her, aside:

DR. HICKENLOOPER
A word, Woodrow. About the settings on the spectrograph. Note: the warning label indicates --

Woodrow follows Dr. Hickenlooper into the tent as she continues to pretend to study/consult about the stolen gear:

DR. HICKENLOOPER
-- the risk of electrocution is sharply increased when --

Dr. Hickenlooper raises an eyebrow. She whispers with authority:

DR. HICKENLOOPER
It's <u>all</u> worthwhile. In your lifetime. <u>This</u>, I mean.

Dr. Hickenlooper refers to the jumble of scientific apparatus (and what it represents to her). Woodrow hesitates.

WOODROW
OK.

DR. HICKENLOOPER
Your curiosity is your most important asset. Trust it.

DR. HICKENLOOPER
Trust your curiosity.

WOODROW
OK.

DR. HICKENLOOPER
The resources of my lab will always be available to you. After this thing is over, I mean. You can sort of be my protégé, if you like.

WOODROW
(pause)
Maybe we can prove the hypothesis of Celestial Flirtation (and get the math right, finally).

DR. HICKENLOOPER
(touched)
Let's try.

WOODROW
(squinting)
I think I see the dots. From space. Burned into your eyeballs.

Woodrow stares into Dr. Hickenlooper's eyes. Long pause.

DR. HICKENLOOPER
I'm sorry about your mother. I miss mine, too. She died forty-six years ago.

WOODROW
(blankly)
Thank you.

Tears stream down Woodrow's face again. Dr. Hickenlooper hugs him.

EXT. MOTEL OFFICE. EVENING

The motel manager stands at the "Deeds" vending machine and makes his pitch to an off-screen customer:

MOTEL MANAGER
I've already petitioned the State Assembly to change the name of the town from "Asteroid City" to "Alien Landing, U.S.A." This municipality might end up being the center of a vast community of -- Stargazers <u>and</u> Space Cadets. It's a historic offering.

CUT TO:

The freckled boy cupping a handful of forty quarters. He bites his lip, weighing his options. His eyes wander to the candy machine.

EXT. METEOR CRATER. EVENING

The entire congregation has re-assembled once more at the bottom/center of the impact crater. Folding chairs. American flag. Cameraman filming. "Asteroid Day" banner (a bit crumpled). The five Junior Stargazers' projects on display. The mechanic stands off to the side holding a small, cardboard box labeled "Unknown." In the audience: Augie's hand is now carefully bandage-wrapped. At his lectern: General Gibson speaks.

GENERAL GIBSON
As you know, the "Asteroid Day" itinerary had to be suspended last week due to the factual reality of -- our circumstances. However: I have an announcement to make. Dr. Hickenlooper and the Military-science Research and Experimentation Division (in conjunction with the Larkings Foundation) have officially selected a recipient for this year's Hickenlooper Scholarship --
(brief/dramatic pause)
-- and you're all going home. First thing tomorrow morning. The president has opted to lift the quarantine (by executive decree).

The group explodes into cheers, applause, hugs, tears. The aide-de-camp appears with the giant-sized $5,000 check. General Gibson says with uneasy warmth/relief:

GENERAL GIBSON
I'd like to take this opportunity -- and, by the way, all of this year's projects (setting aside my own differences of opinion with Ricky Cho) --

General Gibson motions to Ricky, cool but respectful. Ricky nods, also respectful but also cool.

GENERAL GIBSON
-- were of the very highest calibre, without exception -- to formally declare and congratulate the winner of the 1955 Hickenlooper Scholarship --
(hesitates)
What's happening now?

Whispers and murmuring. Everyone has turned to watch: Woodrow, frozen, pointing to the "date" display/scoreboard. He states ominously:

WOODROW
It's today again.

Dr. Hickenlooper frowns. Suddenly: the congregation is illuminated in the familiar green light. They all look up. The spacecraft is hovering silently above. The round hatch on its underside irises open. The alien's scraggly fingers reach out slowly into view, cupping the meteorite in their careful grip, and thrust/toss the rock (as if releasing a bird or butterfly), which then drops straight down, landing with a thump more or less in its original divot. The hatch spirals shut, and the vessel departs exactly as before (with an additional/horizontal loop-de-loop flourish). Everyone stares, mouths open, frozen/agog. Silence. Augie finally clarifies the situation:

AUGIE
I think he only borrowed the asteroid.

INSERT:

The meteorite. General Gibson's hands gingerly touch the surface of the rock, then flip it over to reveal, on the bottom: a hand-painted inventory labeling of indecipherable runic characters. Pause.

GENERAL GIBSON
It's been inventoried.

General Gibson carefully places the rock back in position precisely as it fell. He looks to the business executive, tense. The business executive says immediately:

EXECUTIVE
Re-confiscate the projects.

General Gibson sighs. He strides back to his lectern/microphone to address the group with urgent wariness:

GENERAL GIBSON
Under the provisions of National Security Emergency Scrimmage Plan X: the lifting of the quarantine (which I just announced) is now canceled (or, at least, postponed) due to the unexpected/new event which just --

J.J. zaps the P.A. speaker with Clifford's electromagnetic death-ray. It sizzles/pops/disappears. General Gibson test-taps the dead microphone. The entire congregation erupts into a riot, hurling chairs, knocking over tags and markers, tearing down the banner, etc. Roger rockets up into the air on Ricky's jet-pack, blasting and roaring above the fracas. Sandy throws extraterrestrial rocks at soldiers. J.J. continues to zap pieces of equipment. (Clifford and Shelly egg their parents on. Ricky clings to the rope tether to prevent his father from rocketing into the sky.) Andromeda, Pandora, and Cassiopeia cast spells, swooshing wands, swishing glitter, jumping and shrieking. Stanley laughs hysterically and keeps hold of them by their sleeves, belts, and ribbons. The cowboys and ranch hands swing lassos and holler. The schoolchildren scamper, ecstatic, in every direction as June and the chaperones try to wrangle them. The mechanic yelps as the box in his hands suddenly begins to jump and twist. He drops it on the ground, and the box splits open to reveal the peculiar assembly as it repeats its earlier sputtering, squealing, scooting, etc. Woodrow adjusts a knob on his device/project, gently shielding it from the hubbub. The moon hologram blinks on. Dinah looks up at the sky. Projected on the surface of the actual moon itself: the initials "W.S. + D.C" (inside the outline of a heart-shape). Woodrow and Dinah kiss, a breathless/delirious clutch.

Augie stands immobile at the center of the chaos. He says to Midge, at his side, internal-struggling:

AUGIE
Why does Augie burn his hand on the Quicky-Griddle?
(simply)
I still don't understand the play.

Augie turns and walks briskly to the edge of the crater -- which reveals itself to be a painted backdrop. He opens it (swinging open, along with the rocky terrain, a small section of painted mountains and sky). He exits.

INT. TELEVISION STUDIO. EVENING

Black and white.

The host stands on the theatre proscenium set (now seen from backstage, behind plywood flats mounted on two-by-four joist-frames). A door opens (unfinished plywood on one side, painted crater/mountains/sky on the other) to reveal the actor playing Augie (with bandage-wrapped hand). In the background (onstage): the actors playing Midge, General Gibson, and Dr. Hickenlooper watch, puzzled. Beyond them: footlights and darkness. The actor closes the door.

The host hesitates. He asks the actor:

HOST
Where you going?

ACTOR/AUGIE
(pause)
I'll be right back.

The actor crosses into the wings, past a make-up table where the actor playing the alien is in the process of applying his alien prosthetics. Overheard (with the actress who plays Shelly) as we pass:

ACTOR/ALIEN
I don't play him as an alien, actually. I play him as a metaphor. That's my interpretation.

ACTRESS/SHELLY
(vaguely interested)
Metaphor for what?

ACTOR/ALIEN
(working on it)
I don't know yet.

The actor continues past a live television camera with a confused operator assisted by a puzzled electrician and into the makeshift bedroom installation (unlit) where the director lies sleeping on his folding bunk. The actor stands and says, insistent:

ACTOR/AUGIE
Schubert. Schubert. Schubert.

The lights come up on the set (slightly disorderly: too bright/too dark, blinking on/off) and the director opens his eyes. He bolts upright.

DIRECTOR
Huh? Yes! What's wrong?
(checks his watch)
Are you <u>on</u>?

ACTOR/AUGIE
Technically, but General Gibson just started the scene where the president doesn't accept his resignation. I've got six-and-a-half minutes before my next line. I need an answer to a question I want to ask.

DIRECTOR
(pause)
OK.

ACTOR/AUGIE
Am I doing him right?

Long pause. The director twists and sets his bare feet onto the floor. He answers as he stands up, stretches, then slides a chair from across the room over to the bedside:

DIRECTOR
Well, I told you before: there's too much business. With the pipe, with the lighter, with the camera, with the <u>eyebrow</u>; but, aside from that, on the whole, in answer to your question --

The director directs the actor to sit in the chair. The actor sits. The director kneels on the floor in front of the actor and says, looking into the actor's eyes with his undivided attention:

DIRECTOR
-- you're doing him just right. In fact, in my opinion, you didn't just become Augie: he became you.

ACTOR/AUGIE
I feel lost.

DIRECTOR
Good!

ACTOR/AUGIE
I still don't understand the play.

DIRECTOR
Good!

ACTOR/AUGIE
He's such a wounded guy. He had everything he wanted -- then lost it. Before he even noticed! I feel like my heart is getting broken. My own, personal heart. Every night.

DIRECTOR
Good!

ACTOR/AUGIE
Do I just keep doing it?

DIRECTOR
Yes!

ACTOR/AUGIE
Without knowing anything?

DIRECTOR
Yes!

ACTOR/AUGIE
Isn't there supposed to be some kind of answer? Out there in the cosmic wilderness. Woodrow's line about the meaning of life?

DIRECTOR
"Maybe there is one!"

ACTOR/AUGIE
Right. Well, that's my question. I still don't understand the play.

DIRECTOR
It doesn't matter. Just keep telling the story. You're doing him right.

ACTOR/AUGIE
(pause)
I need a breath of fresh air.

DIRECTOR
(checks his watch)
OK: but you won't find one.

The director crawls back into bed as the actor exits the makeshift bedroom installation. Camera moves past a booth at the stage door, through the exterior wall of the building to:

EXT. ALLEY

Outside in an alley between the docks of two adjacent theatres. (Half-seen marquees read: "Asteroid City" and "Fruit of a Withering Vine.") A delicate snowfall dusts the air. Whizzing taxis zip through the background. The actor closes the stage door and stands on a fire escape a short ladder's flight above a row of trash cans. He takes out Augie's pipe and starts to light it -- then pauses, puts it back into his pocket, and produces a pack of cigarettes, instead. He lights one. An off-screen voice says:

ACTRESS/WIFE (O.S.)
Hello.

The actor looks side to side, up and down, then across the alley -- where he sees, smoking a cigarette on a similar fire escape next to a similar stage door: the actress in the photograph of Woodrow's mother/Augie's deceased wife. She is dressed in Elizabethan costume with starched ruff-collar. The actor hesitates.

ACTOR/AUGIE
Oh! It's you. The wife who played my actress.

The actress nods. Pause.

ACTRESS/WIFE
My scene was cut after one rehearsal.

The actor nods. He shrugs.

ACTOR/AUGIE
We still use your photograph.

The actress thinks. Pause.

ACTRESS/WIFE
Do you remember the dialogue?

The actor thinks. Pause.

ACTOR/AUGIE
No.

The actor and actress puff on their cigarettes. Pause.

ACTRESS/WIFE
We meet in a dream on the alien's planet.

The actor remembers. He nods.

ACTOR/AUGIE
Magnavox-27. Actually, it's one of the moons of it.

Pause. The actress recites (with precision and feeling):

ACTRESS/WIFE
You say: "Did you talk to the alien?" I say: "Not yet." You say: "Why not? I thought for sure you would've yelled at him or made him laugh." I say: "Or asked him the secrets of the universe?" You say: "Exactly!" I say: "I think he's shy." You say: "So's Woodrow, but I'm sure he'll grow out of it. I mean, at least, I hope he will. Without a mother." I say: "He's a late bloomer -- but maybe, I think, you'll need to replace me." You say: "What? Why? How? I can't." I say: "Maybe, I think, you'll need to try. I'm not coming back, Augie." Then you take a picture of me and start crying, and I say: "I hope it comes out."

The actor nods. He remembers the last line:

ACTOR/AUGIE
And I say: "All my pictures come out."
(pause)
Good memory. Why'd they cut it?

ACTRESS/WIFE
(shrugs)
Running time? Now I'm First Lady-in-Waiting to the Queen Consort in "Fruit of a Withering Vine."

The door cracks open. The actor playing the motel manager leans out and says abruptly:

ACTOR/MOTEL MANAGER
You missed your cue! June and the cowboy are already necking in the station wagon. They're bandaging the understudy's hand right now.

The actor throws away his cigarette and darts inside. The door slams behind him. The actor playing the motel manager lingers. He takes out a cigarette and says:

ACTOR/MOTEL MANAGER
Oh! It's you. We almost would've had a scene together. Hello.

Across the alley: the actress nods and smiles as she continues to smoke. Camera leaves her and the actor playing Stanley behind as it dollies away across the television soundstage to:

INT. PLAYWRIGHT'S DESK

Seated at his little desk, clacking at his typewriter, spotlit in the darkness: the playwright. The host, also spotlit, explains:

HOST
Six months into the run, the company received the news: a catastrophic automobile accident. Conrad Earp, American playwright unequaled in passion and imagination, dead at fifty.

The playwright stops typing and looks to camera. Lights/sound slowly fade from him as he speaks -- while, behind him, lights/sound come up on the rehearsal space (Saltzburg Keitel's classroom).

PLAYWRIGHT
I'd like to make a scene where all my characters are each gently/privately seduced into the deepest, dreamiest slumber of their lives as a result of their shared experience of a bewildering and bedazzling celestial mystery...

The students pick up their improvisations exactly where they left off: yawning, snoring, sleepwalking/sleeptalking, tossing and turning, singing a lullaby, thumbsucking with a security blanket, etc. The playwright joins the acting teacher and the director, observing. Eventually, out of the hullaballoo, the actor who plays Augie says from the back of the room:

ACTOR/AUGIE
You can't wake up if you don't fall asleep.

Other actors murmur a response: "What's that mean?" "So what?" "Who said it?" More snoring/tossing/singing, etc. The actress who plays Shelly now says loudly:

ACTRESS/SHELLY
You can't wake up if you don't fall asleep.

Another round of responses, more forceful: "That's not true!" "Who cares?" "Say it again!" The actor who plays the mechanic now says loudly:

ACTOR/MECHANIC
You can't wake up if you don't fall asleep.

The other students, on their feet, raise their voices: "Maybe not?" "Why should you?" "Of course!" The actors who play Roger and Montana shout together:

ACTOR/ROGER
You can't wake up if you don't fall asleep!

ACTOR/MONTANA
You can't wake up if you don't fall asleep!

ACTRESS/MIDGE
(nodding)
You can't wake up if you don't fall asleep!

The teacher's face lights up. He murmurs: "<u>Infinity</u> -- and I don't know what else!" He grabs the playwright's hand and joins the chant, exuberant:

TEACHER
You can't wake up if you don't fall asleep!

The playwright laughs, confused/enchanted. The director and all the other students, jolting from place to place around the room, repeat the chant, first chaotic, then in unison, over and over -- as the alien himself (now fully made-up, with inventoried meteorite tucked under his arm) emerges from the pandemonium (ignored by everyone) and moves to the front of the stage. The lights dim to half-level on the shouting/uproarious classroom with the alien alone in bright spotlight. The host, nearby, watching, turns to camera. He smiles.

EXT. HIGHWAY. DAY

Widescreen/color.

The town: deserted. No barricades. No roadblocks. No guards, cars, jeeps. No press. No public. No vendors, vans, campers. No "Asteroid City Alien Special" passenger train. Only: fluttering litter, empty bottles, and hundreds of tire tracks cross-hatching the barren outskirts. The only remaining people: a crew of two men at work breaking down the Ferris wheel. A single sign on a post has been amended to read:

Strict Quarantine!
LIFTED
by order of
the United States Military-science
Research and Experimentation Division

INT. MOTEL CABINS #9/10. DAY

Cabin #10: the roller-blind zings open once again on Augie's makeshift darkroom. Augie, dressed in pajamas, lights his pipe and looks across/into the bathroom window of Cabin #9. The motel manager (reviewing a clipboard check-list) inspects for dust while a maid (off-screen) runs a vacuum cleaner. The occupants have moved out. Augie squints. He says suddenly:

AUGIE
Where'd they go?

The motel manager looks up. He sees Augie. He smiles and approaches the window as he says brightly:

MOTEL MANAGER
Good morning, Mr. Steenbeck! Juice preference? Apple, orange, or tomato.

AUGIE
(looking left/right)
Where'd they go? Everybody.

MOTEL MANAGER
(hesitates)
Of course, I understand. The president lifted the quarantine, after all. At midnight! He sent the whole gang home. The troops, the cowboys, the Junior Stargazers and Space Cadets. Even the lookie-loos. You're free to return -- back to wherever you came from. (Maybe he's going to change his mind, but nobody stuck around to find out.) We had eleven check-outs this morning.
(cheerily)
I guess you overslept. They returned your science projects, by the way.

The motel manager points to Woodrow's project, boxed/crated, on the doorstep. A label reads: "PROPERTY of the LARKINGS

Foundation (on permanent loan to Woodrow Steenbeck)." Long pause. Augie says finally:

AUGIE
Tomato.

MOTEL MANAGER
Right away!

Camera dollies from Augie's bathroom/darkroom window to his bedroom window. Inside: the three sisters sleep in one bed while Stanley and Woodrow each occupy a folding cot. They are all five sprawled, snoring, tangled in sheets, etc. Augie appears in the doorway and watches/listens for a moment.

EXT. MOTEL CABIN #10. DAY

In the alley behind the cabin: Stanley, also in pajamas, crouching on his knees, attempts to dig in the ground with a gardener's trowel while Andromeda, Pandora, and Cassiopeia, in nightgowns, gasp and shriek, blocking him. The partially unearthed Tupperware salad bowl pokes up from the dirt. Stanley and Woodrow watch, solemn. In the background: Stanley's parked Eldorado. Stanley defends his actions:

STANLEY
The plan was to shovel it up and take her with us. Like I said: we'll <u>exhume</u> the Tupperware. We don't have any burial rights to this plot here.

AUGIE
(interjecting)
I would question whether it even <u>is</u> a plot.

STANLEY
(sharply)
It <u>isn't</u>.

Stanley attempts to resume his digging. The girls, once again, go into a frenzied panic:

CASSIOPEIA
Don't murder my mother's body!

PANDORA
He's killing her ashes!

Stanley stops/freezes. Andromeda commands him:

ANDROMEDA
Let us pray.

Silence. The motel manager appears at some distance with a glass of tomato juice on a tray. He pauses, puzzled. Andromeda screams:

ANDROMEDA

Poppy!

The motel manager disappears. Stanley, spirit crushed, presses on:

STANLEY

Ugh. Dear Heavenly Father, we thank Thee for the life of this magnificent woman, who was once just a little girl like these three -- witches? In-training.

The girls murmur their corrections: "Not in training." "Real witches." "Part-witch, part-alien." Stanley continues:

STANLEY

Like these three witches, at one time. We had no intention of permanently burying her next to this unmarked cactus, but I no longer have the strength to fight for her dignity, nor/neither does Augie. (Do you?)

AUGIE

No.

STANLEY

So we'll defer to the wishes of her stubborn daughters. Woodrow? Any final farewell.

WOODROW

I don't believe in God anymore.

Stanley takes this in stride. He shrugs.

STANLEY

Fair enough. Amen.

"Amens" all around. The three sisters avidly re-bury the Tupperware and stamp down the dusty surface. Tears stream down Stanley's and Augie's faces. Woodrow holds his father's hand. The girls arrange flowers around the gravesite and repeat their whispered incantation: "Friskity, triskity, briskity, boo; knickerty, knockerty, tockerty, too..."

INT. LUNCHEONETTE. DAY

The chime jingles as Augie, Stanley, Woodrow, and the three sisters enter. Augie says to the waitress:

AUGIE

Five orders of flapjacks and two black coffees.

The waitress nods and scribbles. The cook snatches down the order-slip. The family sits.

AUGIE
Who needs to pee?

The girls respond with their unconvincing chorus: "Not me." "I don't." "Nobody needs to pee." The waitress asks them:

WAITRESS
How about a glass of strawberry milk?

The girls perk up. They nod and "uh-huh" eagerly. The waitress sets to work preparing the beverages. The girls change their minds: "I do need to pee." "Where's the powder room?" "Let's go." They scramble away, out the door, around the side of the building. Augie tamps his pipe. Woodrow writes in his notebook. A thought occurs to Stanley:

STANLEY
Did somebody win? That scholarship.

WOODROW
(without looking up)
I did.

AUGIE
(surprised)
When?

WOODROW
Last night. General Gibson slipped it to me in line at the communal showers. I think he just wanted to get it over with. It's actually a standard-sized check of typical dimensions. The big one's only for show.

Woodrow digs into his pocket. He produces/hands over a normal-sized check for $5000. Augie says, enormously excited:

AUGIE
Congratulations, Woodrow. That's stupendous!

STANLEY
(deeply impressed)
You must be some kind of genius.

AUGIE
I agree.

STANLEY
(rephrasing it)
You must be some kind of -- "Brainiac."

Woodrow smiles, good-natured, and goes back to his notebook. Stanley stares at the check for a moment and asks:

STANLEY
Has it got any strings attached to it? It's made out to you, personally. How you plan to use it?

Woodrow takes back the check. He examines it. He shrugs.

WOODROW
Probably spend it on my girlfriend.

Woodrow re-pockets the check and returns to his notebook. Augie and Stanley exchange a look. Stanley asks Woodrow, curious:

STANLEY
What do you write? In that little book.

Woodrow looks at Stanley briefly (not sure he can trust him). He shows him a page.

WOODROW
Next year's project. Confidentially.

Stanley and Augie study the notebook. They look utterly fascinated. They mutter simultaneously, concentrating:

AUGIE
Wow. Is that possible?

STANLEY
Gee whiz. Look at that.

Woodrow withdraws the notebook suddenly. He resumes his work. The waitress appears with a little slip of paper (folded in half) which she slides to Augie.

WAITRESS
Midge Campbell left you her address. (It's just a post office box.)

Augie raises an eyebrow. He nods. He opens the slip of paper and reads. He and Stanley exchange another/different look. Stanley leans to Augie and whispers something inaudible into his ear. Augie says, taken aback:

AUGIE
That's none of your business, Stanley.

STANLEY
I know. Of course, it isn't. (I only ask because Woodrow told me Dinah told him.)
(more)

STANLEY (cont'd)
I went to law school with her former agent. Anyway: I don't object.
(encouraging)
She's actually a very gifted comedienne.

Long pause. Augie says sadly/gladly/genuinely:

AUGIE
That's true.

A distant boom shudders the building (once again). Only Stanley reacts, alarmed. Down the counter, the cashier dismisses the matter:

CASHIER
Another atom bomb test.

Stanley hesitates. He nods slowly. Breakfast continues.

EXT. HIGHWAY. DAY

The blacktop interstate. At the meteor crater: the radio telescopes continue their perpetual spinning. At the filling station: there are now two station wagons on blocks in the adjacent small junkyard. At the chopped-off elevated highway-spur: the sounds of approaching sirens, motors, gunshots; then the Chevy (still dragging its muffler, which pops off and spirals into the air) roars through, down the highway, pursued by the state trooper and motorcycle police. At the motor court hotel: the gardener/handyman finishes replacing the letters on his sign which now reads: "Welcome to Alien Landing, U.S.A. Limited quantity of land parcels still available." (In the background, beyond the mountains, a mushroom cloud lingers in the sky.) At the luncheonette: Augie, Stanley, Woodrow, and the three girls climb into the Eldorado, now overflowing with boxes and luggage. The waitress, standing in the doorway, drying her hands on her apron, nods goodbye.

At the railroad crossing, beyond the covered-wagon sign: the warning bell rings as a freight train passes through (opposite direction from opening scene); and finally the Eldorado pulls up, waits for the caboose to clear, then drives away, into the hot desert.

Additional Scene

INT. ELEMENTARY SCHOOL. DAY

A burnished Arts-and-Crafts-period classroom in a medium-sized small town with orange/avocado trees and whirring lawnmowers outside. The walls are filled with alien-related ephemera: drawings and paintings in every medium; *papiers maché* planets and spacecraft; a diagrammed sentence on the chalkboard which refers to stolen/returned asteroid. The host (standing behind the last row of desks) explains:

HOST

A mimeographed *coda* to "Asteroid City" was discovered papering the insulation of the attic of the playwright's winter residence. It takes place in late spring, one half-year subsequent to the events depicted in the play's original production.

June addresses her students:

JUNE

These vast molecular clouds of cosmic dust and interstellar gasses (known as nebulae) then cool and coalesce to form stars or planets or other wildly diverse celestial --

Dwight, pointing out the window, interrupts:

DWIGHT

Lookit! Who's here.

Across the road, the cowboy troupe (lighting cigarettes) steps down from a chartered Greyhound hand-painted broadside: MONTANA AND THE RANCH HANDS featuring "Dance The Spaceman" (with regional tour dates listed below). June's heart sinks/leaps. Bootsteps come to a stop outside the open door to the corridor. June turns again and stares. Her voice breaks slightly:

JUNE

Yes, Montana?

Montana removes his hat as he drifts into the classroom. He begins, cheery/humble but uneasy:

MONTANA

Howdy, Dwight. Howdy, rest a' y'all.
Howdy, June.

JUNE

(evenly)

Howdy.

MONTANA
The boys and m'self happened to be a'passin' through town on our way to the music hall yonder up the road a piece. Actually, a <u>bit</u> of a detour. (350 miles.) We thought we'd mosey over and share this commem'rative pressin' a' Dwight's alien song --
(significantly)
-- and a royalty check.

Montana displays a 45rpm single (featuring Dwight standing on Montana's shoulders, hands on hips). He presents an envelope to Dwight. Dwight rips it open and registers the amount.

DWIGHT
Yow! I'm rich. Miss Douglas?

June hesitates. She nods. Dwight dashes over to put the disc onto the classroom record player. The other pupils gather to listen while Montana automatically follows June back out into the corridor (which is also filled with aliens up and down the walls from more grades and classes). June pulls the door quietly shut while the song plays inside. Pause.

JUNE
Congratulations on your success. My word.

MONTANA
You got m'letters, a'course?

JUNE
(hesitates)
Of course. I wrote you.

MONTANA
(not annoyed)
Once.

JUNE
(not guilty)
Once.

Montana hands June a small, slightly crushed pink flower. June nods.

JUNE
Bitterroot.

Montana shrugs and shuffles. He smiles briefly.

MONTANA
Seven months a'passed.

JUNE
(pause)
Yes.

Montana and June watch each other carefully for a moment. Montana says finally:

MONTANA
Seven months, two weeks, three days; and now I have the <u>means</u>, you see; so I thought to propose, though I know it ain't likely, but I figgered I ought to take my chances; how to put it? Would you care to --
(long pause)
-- "be mine"?

Montana descends onto one knee. June's mouth falls slowly open. Montana sheepishly produces a box. Which he opens. It appears to contain a ring. June descends to one knee, as well. She closes the little box and says as gently as possible:

JUNE
No.

MONTANA
Well, that ain't open to any misinturpurtation. There's m'answer.

JUNE
If you please: I don't mean my "no" as a -- personal rejection, Montana. I mean it as the expression of something <u>I don't want</u>. At this time or, perhaps, ever.

MONTANA
(trying to understand)
You don't want --

Montana points to himself as June responds simultaneously:

JUNE
To be anybody's. Let's stop kneeling.

June takes Montana's hand and holds it. They stand.

JUNE
I don't know that I can explain myself better than to say: I have other -- very vague -- but very <u>definite</u> -- ideas --
(almost inaudible)
-- about my future.

MONTANA
Yep. I follow your logic there. I reckon that'll be a firm "no", in that case, I reckon.

JUNE
Yes.

MONTANA
I understand. I'm awful sorry to a' sprung up on you like this. Out of the goosegrass. It's just, well, my heart feels like a mule kicked it; and the fellers tell me I done part-near lost the power a' speech; and the world's a big, wide-open, right beauteous ole place (and so's the universe, for that matter) -- but I don't know where to be in it no more, June. What else to do but appear on your doorstep even though I tole myself again and again: there's no hope in it a'tall.
(desolate)
And there ain't.

A third party has appeared. The school's principal and head-mistress, Mrs. Wheatcroft. She says, warm but authoritative:

PRINCIPAL
Good afternoon.

JUNE
(startled)
Good afternoon, Mrs. Wheatcroft. This is my -- cousin -- Montana. Montana, this is our school's principal, Mrs. --

PRINCIPAL
(immediately intrigued)
With the singing troupe? "Montana and the Ranch Hands".

MONTANA
Yes, ma'am.

PRINCIPAL
Dwight's song!

MONTANA
Yes, ma'am.

Mrs. Wheatcroft looks from Montana to June to Montana to June. Montana pockets the ring-box. Mrs. Wheatcroft issues a command:

PRINCIPAL
Young man! Play for us.

JUNE
(lost)
Oh. I think --

PRINCIPAL
Music class starts in three minutes.

JUNE
-- the band's travel schedule --

PRINCIPAL
Nonsense. I insist.

June, upset, attempts to rescue Montana while Montana, detached, nods and consents to the principal's request:

JUNE
Montana. Don't feel obligated.

MONTANA
Surely. Surely. Surely, ma'am.

CUT TO:

Three minutes later. Back inside the classroom. The students listen as the cowboy troupe plays and harmonizes to "Streets of Laredo". Mrs. Wheatcroft accompanies them on the upright piano. Montana sings bleakly. June stares off into space. (A cosmic/interstellar map behind her underscores the vastness of her gloom.) The host (waiting in the corridor) eventually resumes:

HOST
"The Ranch Hands", as they had come to be known, performed a brief recital of five songs for Mrs. Wheatcroft's music class before departing for their concert in eastern Nevada -- but the characters of Montana and June were never (in life or art) afforded the opportunity to speak to each other again.

ASTEROID CITY

Gallery of Images

THEATRE
SALTZBURG KEITEL THEATRE
VARIETY

GAS
SERVICE STATION

FRENCH PRESS

CANDY
SNACKS
REAL ESTATE
MILK
SOUP
TOILETRIES
Campbell's
SOUPS
ICE
ICE

1st REHEARSAL
Cast call: 8am Sharp
--Mr. Greene (Director)

SOAPY

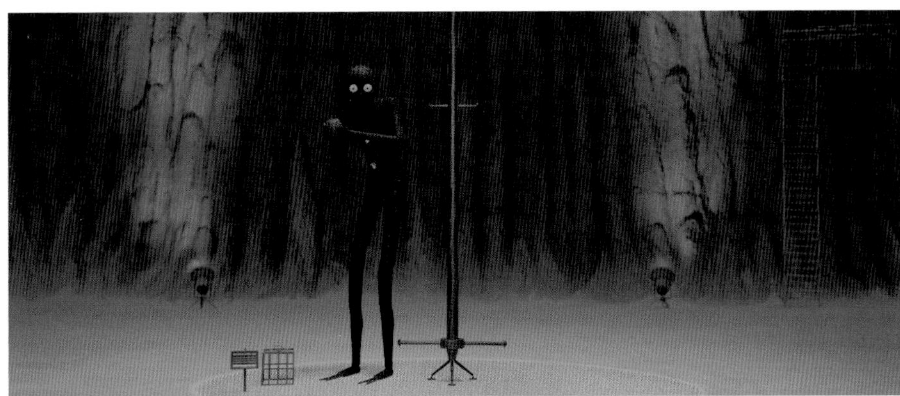

CAFE
BREAKFAST
LUNCHEON
HOT SUPPER
BEEF PORK
FRIED CHICKEN
SODA FOUNTAIN
COLD DRINKS
HOME MADE PIES
SPARE RIBS
SODA POP LEMONADE 5¢
HAM PLATE
EGGS BACON HOTCAKES 50¢
CHILI BEANS 35¢
PORK CHOPS
BAKED HAM 50¢
BUS DEPOT

Oil

QUARANTINE
QUARANTINE
ASTEROID
CITY
DOOMS
DAY
Do Not Enter (Or Exit)